# FAMOUS TRAVELLERS TO THE HOLY LAND

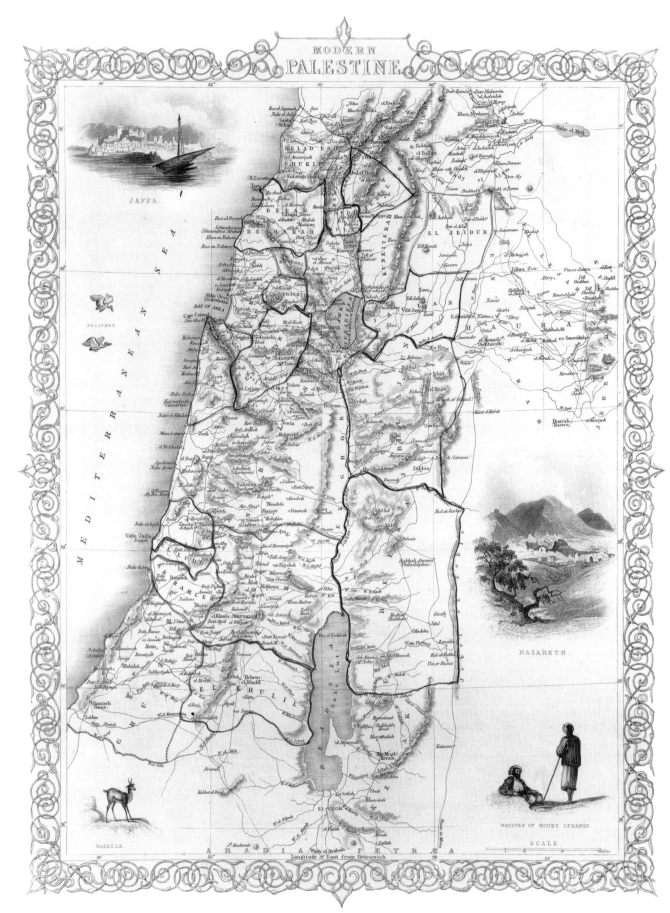

Map of Palestine, 1851 (steel engraving by J. Tallin)

# FAMOUS TRAVELLERS TO THE HOLY LAND

*Their Personal
Impressions and Reflections*

Compiled by
LINDA OSBAND

With an Introduction by
JAN MORRIS

**PRION**

First published in the United Kingdom 1989 by
**PRION**
An imprint of Multimedia Books Limited
32/34 Gordon House Road
London NW5 1LP

Editor: Linda Osband
Design: Behram Kapadia
Picture research: Linda Osband

British Library Cataloguing in Publication Data
Famous travellers to the Holy Land.
1. Palestine. Description & travel history
I. Osband, Linda
915.694

ISBN 1 85375 031 X

Typeset and originated by Wyvern Typesetting Limited, Bristol, UK
Printed in Spain by Imago Publishing

# Contents

# INTRODUCTION
## by Jan Morris

To describe what used to be called Palestine, the Holy Land, as one of the two or three supreme destinations of the world is perhaps an understatement. The thirteenth-century Mappa Mundi at Hereford, our greatest surviving medieval map, shows Jerusalem its capital actually at the centre of the world, surrounded deferentially by all the seas and continents. To devotees of two religions, Judaism and Christianity, the Holy Land is the moral focus of all things – 'Next year in Jerusalem!' say the Jews in yearning for it, 'Jerusalem My Happy Home', blithely sing the Christians, To followers of a third, Islam, it is a place of sanctity hardly less intense; to them Jerusalem is El Quds, the Holy, and from its Stone of Paradise, the Foundation of the World, Mohammed the Prophet ascended to heaven. All three religions see Palestine as a chosen land, and Jerusalem as more than just a city, but a figure of the celestial, perfection's prototype.

No modern map projection can honestly represent Jerusalem as the heart of the world: at 31.47N, 35.13E, set on a high austere plateau in territory in more or less constant dispute, it is remote from the great power sources of our time, and peripheral to the great events. Nor is it a major metropolis, having a population of only half a million. But now as ever, it and its surrounding countryside possesses a significance and an allure far beyond its size and material importance. Call it what you will – Palestine, Israel, Holy Land – this is the most allegorical of all countries. Conquerors of many ages, many nationalities, have counted it their noblest objective, not because it commands strategic routes or economic resources, but because it is so charged with meaning. Arabs, Crusaders, Israelis have fought for it with a unique passion.

Through it all the country, and especially Jerusalem at the heart of it, inspired passionate loyalties – passionate hatreds too – and it remained always, as it remains today, a place of constant pilgrimage. Some of its visitors went there because it was beautiful. Others went because it was a fascinating flashpoint of history, or an adventurous place to wander. Most travellers made the journey, though, because of its holiness – not necessarily because they were religious people themselves, but because they felt the tug of its innate sanctity and its divine reputation. Our book honours all these purposes of travel, but it is to Palestine as Holy Land to which it chiefly takes us.

The pilgrims whose memoirs it includes all came from the West – another book altogether could be compiled about travellers from the other half of the world – and they were of very varied background. We have observers from America, France, Austria, Ireland and England. We have a poet, a diplomat, a novelist, a naturalist, a couple of generals, a king's wife and a missionary. We have Edward Lear, Mark Twain, Oscar Wilde's father and the doomed Rudolph, Crown Prince of Austria. Most of the travellers went to Palestine in the second half of the nineteenth century, and by the nature of things most of them were people of privilege – for until the age of the package tour a journey to the Holy Land was an expensive project.

Do not expect their responses to be all pious exclamation. Some are disrespectful of what they find, others are taken aback – it is an old Protestant tradition, in particular, to be shocked by the factional divisions of Jerusalem. Throughout the nineteenth century the Turks remained suzerains of the Holy Land, and these fastidious and cultivated visitors from the West were often affronted by the fact, partly on religious grounds but partly because they despised administrative incompetence. They were frequently sceptical, too, about supposed relics or miraculous events, they resented the tourist exploitation of foreigners, and more than one thought the appearance of Jerusalem extremely disappointing – no more than 'a walled town of the third or fourth class', says James Silk Buckingham.

We find the future Lord Kitchener having a boy publicly flogged for stone-throwing. We find Edward Lear with a 'very filthy and incapable' escort. John Macgregor is not pleased to encounter, in the public baths at Tiberias, 'a number of naked and moist negroes', and Laurence Oliphant considers an early experiment in Arab–Jewish co-operation 'more picturesque than satisfactory'.

Few of these worldly travellers, then, are sycophantic, still less hypocritical. They are generally frank enough about their experiences, and often disconcerting. Hardly one of them, though, fails to respond to the innate grandeur of the country they are visiting. At the back of almost all their minds, whether they are conducting a military survey, or directing an archaeological dig, or simply making an adventurous journey, is the knowledge that they are on sacred ground. This is travel writing of a very particular kind – writing animated, whether consciously or not, by the spirituality of place.

One might not expect Mark Twain, that most irrepressible of humorists, to be the most articulate about such an experience, but in fact I think his memoir best expresses what so many of his colleagues feel. He was half-amused, half-repelled to find a grotto in Nazareth purported to be the Virgin Mary's sitting-room; he was disappointed to discover the River Jordan by no means (as he had assumed since boyhood) 4,000 miles long and 35 miles wide; he was depressed by the dreary wretchedness, dirt and poverty of Turkish Palestine. But he knew himself always, even in his laughter and contempt, to be in a grand and holy place: and the thoughts that Jerusalem itself suggested to him were, as he nobly says, thoughts 'full of poetry, sublimity, and more than all, dignity'.

Such is the *genius loci* of the Holy Land, and such is the message, often concealed between heedless, bitter or merely entertaining lines, of this very special book of travels.

'In most European countries travellers are enabled by the modern facilities for locomotion, and with the aid of timetables, to mete out their time to the best possible advantage, and to apportion each day and even hour with tolerable precision; but the traveller in the still semi-barbarous East must be content with framing a more general plan for his tour, and must leave the minuter details to be filled in according to circumstances as he proceeds on his way. In Syria the horse affords the only mode of conveyance, except for long journeys through the desert, when the camel is chiefly used.... The country cannot boast of a single carriage-road, except those from Jaffa to Jerusalem and from Beirut to Damascus, far less a railway; and the success of a tour is therefore dependent on the health and energy of the traveller, on the weather, and on a host of incidental circumstances which do not occur in Europe....'

'The word *bakshish*, which resounds so perpetually in the traveller's ears during his sojourn in the East, and haunts him long afterwards, simply means "a gift", and as everything is to be had for gifts the word has many different applications. Thus with bakshish the tardy operations of the custom-house officer are accelerated, bakshish supplies the place of a passport, bakshish is the alms bestowed on a beggar, bakshish means blackmail, and lastly a large proportion of the public officials of the country are said to live almost exclusively on bakshish.'

From Baedeker's *Palestine and Syria: Handbook for Travellers*, 1876

# JAMES TURNER BARCLAY

## 1807–74

*James Turner Barclay*

*James Turner Barclay was an American physician and missionary who was active in Jerusalem from 1851 to 1854. This was the period of the first American religious colonists, who went to the Holy Land with the intention of converting the Jews to Christianity. As they had been unsuccessful, a new society, the American Christian Missionary Society, decided in 1851 to start its own campaign under Barclay's direction. During his three years in Palestine, he not only tried to undertake this missionary work, but he also succeeded in discovering part of ancient Jerusalem and elucidating some of the questions concerning the topography and archaeology of the ancient city. By managing to cure the Turkish effendi of 'a disagreeable affection', he also managed to obtain a special firman to enter the ancient Temple area, becoming one of the first Christians to be allowed to explore and measure it. The results of his observations and reflections were published on his return to Philadelphia in 1858 in The City of the Great King, which was hailed as a major contribution to biblical literature.*

*Discovery of a Subterranean Quarry, Jerusalem*

Having received some intimation of the existence of an entrance to a very extensive cave near the Damascus Gate (entirely unknown to Franks), we resolved upon its exploration, on the strength of the nazir's permission. Accordingly, a few days afterwards, father, brother and myself repaired thither; and after several hours of vain labour, finding it utterly impossible to effect an entrance unperceived in the open light of day, we concluded to return in the shades of evening – resolving to pass the night under Jerusalem in making a thorough exploration.

Having provided ourselves with all the requisites for such a furtive adventure – matches, candles, compass, tape-line, paper and pencils – a little previous to the time of closing the gates of the city, we sallied out at different points, the better to avoid exciting suspicion, and rendezvoused at Jeremiah's Pool, near to which we secreted ourselves within a white enclosure surrounding the tomb of a departed Arab sheikh, until the shades of darkness enabled us to approach unperceived – when we issued from our hiding-place, amid the screeching of owls, screaming of hawks, howling of jackals and the chirping of nocturnal insects. The mouth of the cavern being immediately below the city wall and the houses of Bezetha, we proceeded cautiously in the work of removing the dirt, mortar and stones; and, after undermining and picking awhile, a hole ... was made, though scarcely large enough for us to worm our way serpentinely through the ten-foot wall.

On scrambling through and descending the inner side of the wall, we found our way apparently obstructed by an immense mound of soft dirt, which had been thrown in, the more effectually to close up the entrance; but, after examining awhile, discovered that it had settled down in some places sufficiently to allow us to crawl over it on hand and knee; which, having accomplished, we found ourselves enveloped in thick darkness, that might be felt, but not penetrated by all our lights, so vast is the hall.

For some time we were almost overcome with feelings of awe and admiration (and I must say apprehension, too, from the immense impending vaulted roof), and felt quite at a loss to decide in which direction to wend our way. There is a constant and in many places very rapid descent from the entrance to the termination, the distance between which two points, in a nearly direct line, is 750 feet; and the cave is upwards of 3,000 feet in circumference, supported by great numbers of rude natural pillars. At the southern extremity there is a very deep and precipitous pit, in which we received a very salutary warning of caution from the dead – a human skeleton!...There is also near this pit a basin excavated in the solid rock about five feet in diameter and two and a half feet deep, into which the percolating water trickles; but it was in vain we tried to quench our thirst with water of such bitter, disagreeable taste. A little, however, was bottled for analysis....

...Numerous crosses marked on the wall indicated that, though unknown to Christendom of the present day, the devout pilgrim or crusader had been there; and a few Arabic and Hebrew inscriptions (though too much effaced to be deciphered) proved that the place was not unknown to the Jew and Arab. Indeed, the manner in which the beautiful white solid limestone rock was everywhere carved by the mason's rough chisel into regular pillars, proved that this extensive cavern, though in part natural, was formerly used as the grand quarry of Jerusalem....

Though disappointed in our fond expectations of working our way to the Sanctum Sanctorum, Hippicus or Antonia, as we had vaguely conjectured we might be enabled to do, we were nevertheless highly delighted with our little jaunt in nether Jerusalem.

*Noble Sanctuary*

There is no place on earth concerning which there has existed a curiosity half so intense and prurient as that in relation to the sacred enclosure of the Temple, the Haram es-Sherif, which can only perish with the faith it typifies. But so great is the fear inspired by the clubs and scimitars of those blood-thirsty savages, the Mauritanian Africans, to whose jealous custody the entire Haram is committed, that few indeed have been found of sufficient temerity to hazard even the most furtive and cursory reconnaissance of this tabooed spot. It is an ascertained fact that every religious community in the Holy City has a firman from the Sublime Porte empowering them to kill the members of any other communities intruding on their premises; and that the Moslems, at least, delight to execute the decree upon any infidel, whether Jew or Christian, that may be caught intruding upon this sacred spot, is well known....

A most fortunate circumstance, however, soon [occurred]. The sultan's architect, having petitioned the Mejlis of Jerusalem for permission to associate me with him in designing the proposed improvements about the Haram, procured my official and unrestricted admittance to every part of the sacred enclosure, both above and below ground, without fee or reward.

I was not even required to undergo the important ecclesiastical lustration by water on the occasion. In order, however, to avoid the appearance of anything that would savour of the observance of a Mohammedan rite, I took care to go voluntarily and submit to the rubbing, scrubbing, bumping, thumping, racking, cracking operation of the Turkish bath, so as to forestall all difficulties on the score of uncleanness....

But however anxious to explore the mysteries of that sacred spot, I was fully resolved to submit to none of the degrading ceremonies to which Christian and Jewish mechanics had been required heretofore to do on entering the Haram for the purpose of making repairs. It is well known that every kind of handicraft avocation is regarded as degrading by all classes of Moslems; and hence when the clock of the mosque needs repairing, they are compelled, however reluctantly, to employ a Frank. But in order to have a clean conscience of such an abominable piece of sacrilege as the admission of an infidel upon the sacred premises, they adopt the following expedient. The mechanic selected being thoroughly purged from his uncleanness by ablution *à la Turk*, a certain formula of prayer and incantation is sung over him at the gate. This being satisfactorily concluded, he is considered as exorcised, not only of Christianity (or Judaism, as the case may be), but of humanity also; and is declared to be no longer a man but a donkey. He is then mounted upon the shoulders of the faithful lest, notwithstanding his depuration, the ground should be polluted by his footsteps; and being carried to the spot where his labours are required, he is set down upon matting within certain prescibed limits; and the operation being performed, he is carried back to the gate, and there, by certain other ceremonies, he is duly undonkeyfied and transmuted into a man again!...

The enclosure of the Haram es-Sherif, or the Noble Sanctuary, as the area of the Temple is now called, contains about thirty-six acres. The east side of this large quadrilateral enclosure runs due north and south, but no other side is either perpendicular or parallel to it, nor any two sides the same length ... such is the nature of the ground, and such the difficulties arising from impenetrable copses of cactus, interposing buildings and accumulations of rubbish that error [in its measurement] is unavoidable; and no measurement that is practicable to make can be regarded as absolutely reliable.... Though I found no difficulty in measuring and drawing anything out of sight of the Mugrabin guard, entirely at my leisure,

*The Mosque of Omar on the ancient site of the Temple, by David Roberts*

yet I had no sooner commenced measuring the area of the Haram than the effendi took alarm at the fanatical demonstration of the guard, and we deemed it prudent to desist for a while, in the hope that they would become better reconciled.

The surface of this enclosure is by no means a uniform plane, there being a general declination towards the south and east. The ground immediately south of the Golden Gate is quite low, that around Solomon's Throne is elevated, and the rock surface in the north-west corner is considerably higher than any other part of the area – the platform of course excepted....

The Golden Gate is situated $456\frac{1}{4}$ feet from the north-east corner of the Haram. It is fifty-five feet in width and projects about six. It was through this gate, tradition says, the Son of David made his triumphant entry into the city, and through it the Emperor Heraclius also entered triumphantly, bearing the Cross, which he had recovered from the Persians.

Whether it was blocked up by Christians or Moslems is uncertain; but evident it is that the latter are well content to let it remain closed, having the fear of the Bedouin as well as the Christian before their eyes.

All the gates of the city are scrupulously kept closed for an hour or two every Friday (the Mohammedan Sabbath), because of a universal belief that an attempt will, sooner or later, be made by Christians to take the city at Friday noon....

Pursuing our survey around the patched walls of the Temple, on the south, we observe, amongst its cyclopean masonry, immediately west of the Triple Gate, a stone, four feet wide and five and three-quarters long, standing on end – being built perpendicularly into the wall. It has a beautiful moulding on one edge and probably once formed part of the decoration around the top of the old Temple wall, which Josephus says 'was of excellent workmanship upwards and around the top of it'.... The observant traveller will not fail to scan it with a critical eye. Just above the right hand upper corner of the subterranean gateway lintel at the junction of the city and Temple walls, we find another proof of the hasty and imperfect manner in which this wall has been rebuilt, in the inverted inscription of one of its stones. Some of the letters are nearly effaced by the erosive influence of time and the elements....From this inscription it may safely be inferred that the wall was rebuilt at a period somewhat posterior to Antonius Pius. At the south-west corner these colossal blocks of stone are found still larger than those at the other corners, as might be reasonably inferred from the vicinity of the immense bridge, probably just as they were placed by the architect of Solomon or his immediate successor. They vary in size from five to six and a quarter feet in thickness, and from twenty to thirty feet in length. Nearly all of the upper part of the wall, however, is rather indifferently constructed of small stones....

At the 'Wailing Place' ... these large rocks are again visible, and in the pool beneath the causeway they are in fine preservation; but the rest of the wall is concealed by houses as far as the Moat of Antonia, beyond which the wall is constructed of much smaller stones until it unites with the tower at the north-east corner....

A few of these lower tiers of stones have lain many centuries inhumed. And there is no proof that some of them have ever been removed from the position in which they were first placed: but this cannot justly be construed into a non-fulfilment of our Saviour's prophecy, recorded by Luke (xix. 44) in relation to the stones of the city. That relating to the Temple itself (Matt. xxiv. 2) has been so completely and literally fulfilled that, so far as is known, not a single stone of the 'magnifical' building is left in situ. That in Luke has been fulfilled in spirit, just as completely – the enemy did lay the devoted city even with the ground, and her children within her – in the sense intended; and in the same sense, 'not one stone was left upon another', and yet no doubt there were millions of stones actually lying one upon another in every part of the city!...

# GERTRUDE BELL

## 1868–1926

*Gertrude Bell, 1887 (portrait by Flora Russell)*

*Gertrude Bell was born on 14 July 1868 in Co. Durham and was educated at Lady Margaret Hall, Oxford, becoming the first woman candidate to obtain a first-class degree in modern history in 1888. Her love of travel began early – she went to Romania at twenty-two – and, after having studied Persian, she wrote one of her best-known books,* Safar Nameh: Persian Pictures, *in 1894. Her true love of the East was awakened in 1899, when she settled for the winter in Jerusalem in order to study Arabic, and adventurous visits to Petra and Baalbek led to an enthusiasm for desert travel and Syrian archaeology. In 1905 she set out on a journey through Syria to Konia in Asia Minor, her vivid account of it,* The Desert and the Sown, *being published in 1907. Her description of her journey to Ukhaidir in 1911,* The Palace and the Mosque of Ukhaidir, *became her most important archaeological publication. In 1915 her knowledge of the desert Arabs and Middle East politics led to her recruitment to the Arab Bureau in Cairo and, in 1917, to her appointment as Oriental Secretary to the British High Commissioner in Baghdad, where she stayed for the rest of her life. In 1927, a year after her death, a two-volume selection of her letters was published.*

*Jericho*
*17 January 1900*

I rode down here yesterday afternoon with Isa, one of the kavasses. We started at 1.30 and got here at 5, which was pretty good going. It was a most pleasant day for riding, cool and not sunny, today is brilliantly sunny. I came down the last hill in company with a band of Turkish soldiers, ragged, footsore, weary, poor dears! but cheerful. We held a long conversation. The Russian Pilgrim House we visited last night and found it packed with pilgrims as tight as herrings sleeping in rows on the floor. Even the courtyard was quite full of them and on a tree an eikon round which a crowd of them were praying. Charlotte [Roche, a childhood friend] and I rode off with Isa about 11 and went down to the Jordan, taking our lunch with us. There we found an enormous crowd assembled. Bedouin and fellaheen, kavasses in embroidered clothes. Turkish soldiers, Greek priests and Russian peasants, some in furs and top boots and some in their white shrouds, which were to serve as bathing dresses in the holy stream and then to be carried home and treasured up till the owner's death. We lunched and wandered about for some time, I photographing some of these strange groups – long-haired Russian priests in their shrouds standing praying in the hot sun by the river bank, among the tamarisk bushes and the reeds, every one, men and women, had chains of beads and crucifixes hung round their necks. The sun was very hot and we waited and waited while those who were going to be baptized signed their names and paid a small fee. We found ourselves ensconced on willow boughs just opposite to the place where the priests were coming down to bless the water. We waited for about half an hour, then the crowd opened and a long procession of priests came to the water's edge with lighted candles. The shrouded people clambered down the mud banks and stood waist deep in the stream until the moment when the priest laid the cross three times upon the water, then suddenly, with a great firing off of guns, everyone proceeded to baptize himself by dipping and rolling over in the water. It was the strangest sight. Some of them had hired monks at a small fee to baptize them and they certainly got their money's worth of baptism, for the monks took an infinite pleasure in throwing them over backwards into the muddy stream and holding them under until they were quite saturated. We then rowed back, returned to our horses and got back about 5.

*Desert Excursion from Jerusalem*
*Tuesday, 20 March 1900*

*From my tent*

I left Jerusalem yesterday soon after 9.... I rode down to Jerusalem alone – the road was full of tourists, caravans of donkeys carrying tents for cook and Bedouin escorts. I made friends as I went along and rode with first one Bedouin and then another, all of them exaggerating the dangers I was about to run with the hope of being taken with me into Moab.... I determined to pass that night in Jericho and make an early start.

This morning I got up at 5 and at 6 was all ready, having sent on my mules and Hanna [the cook] to the Jordan bridge.... The river valley is wider on the other side and was full of tamarisks in full white flower and willows in the newest of leaf, there were almost no slime pits and when we reached the level of the Ghor (that is the Jordan plain) behold, the wilderness had blossomed like the rose. It was the most unforgettable sight – sheets and sheets of varied and exquisite colour – purple, white, yellow and the brightest blue – (this was a bristly sort of plant which I don't know) and fields of scarlet ranunculus. Nine-tenths of them I didn't know, but there was the yellow daisy, the sweet-scented mauve wild stock, a great splendid sort of dark purple onion, the white garlic and purple mallow, and higher up a tiny blue iris and red anemones and a dawning pink thing like a linum.

We had now reached the bottom of the foot-hills, and leaving the Ghor behind us, we began to mount. We crossed a stream flowing down the Wady Hisban (which is Heshbon of the fish-pools in the Song of Songs) at a place called Akweh. It was so wet here that we rode on to a place where there were a few thorn trees peopled by immense crowds of resting birds – they seize on any little bush for there are so few and the Arabs come and burn the bush and catch and cook the birds all in one! On the top of the first shoulder we came to spreading cornfields. The plan is this – the 'Arabs' sow one place this year and go and live somewhere else lest their animals should eat the growing corn. Next year this lies fallow and the fallow of the year before is sown. Over the second shoulder we got on to a stretch of rolling hills and we descended the valley to Ain Mousa, a collection of beautiful springs with an Arab camp pitched above them. I found the loveliest iris I have yet seen – big and sweet-scented and so dark purple that the hanging down petals are almost black. It decorates my tent now. Half an hour later my camp was pitched a little lower down on a lovely grassy plateau. We were soon surrounded by Arabs who sold us a hen and some excellent sour milk, 'laban' it is called. While we bargained the women and children wandered round and ate grass, just like goats. The women are unveiled. They wear a blue cotton gown six yards long which is gathered up and bound round their heads and their waists and falls to their feet. Their faces, from the mouth downwards, are tattooed with indigo and their hair hangs down in two long plaits on either side....We saw a great flock of storks today (the Father of Luck, Tarif calls them) and an eagle. I am now amongst the Bilka Arabs but these particular people are the Ghanimat, which Hanna explains as Father of Flocks.

*Thursday 22:* This has been a most wonderful day. Hanna woke me at 5.30. By 6.30 I had breakfasted and was ready to start. I sent up to know if my soldier was coming. He arrived in a few minutes, a big handsome cheerful Circassian mounted on a strong white horse, and a little before 7 we started off. In a dip we came suddenly upon a great encampment of Christians from Madeba and stopped to photograph them and their sheep. They were milking them, the sheep being tied head to head in a serried line of perhaps forty at a time. We went on and on, the ground rising and falling and always the same beautiful grass – no road, we went straight across country. Another big encampment of Christians. The people were most friendly and one man insisted on mounting his little mare and coming with us, just for love. So we all cantered off together, through many flocks and past companies of dignified storks walking about and eating locusts, till we came to the road, the pilgrim road to Mecca. Road of course it is not; it is about one-eighth of a mile wide and consists of hundreds of parallel tracks trodden out by the immense caravan which passes over it twice a year. We next came to some camps and flocks of the Beni Sakhr, the most redoubted of all the Arab tribes and the last who submitted to the Sultan's rule – 'Very much not pleasant,' said Tarif – and now we were almost at the foot of the low hills and before us stood the ruins of Mashetta. It is a Persian palace, begun and never finished by Chosroes I, who overran the country in 611 of our era and planned to have a splendid hunting box in there. Grassy plains which abound in game. The beauty of it all was quite past words. It's a thing one will never forget as long as one lives. At last, most reluctantly, we turned back on our four hours' ride home. We hadn't gone more than a few yards before three of the Beni Sakhr came riding towards us, armed to the teeth, black browed and most menacing. When they saw our soldier they threw us the salaam with some disgust, and after a short exchange of politenesses, proceeded on their way – we felt that the interview might have turned

*Russian pilgrims preparing for the Epiphany ceremony at the River Jordan*

differently if we had been unescorted. We rode on straight across the plains putting up several foxes and a little grey wolf. Unfortunately we did not see the white gazelles of which there are said to be many, also jackals – and hyenas. Just as we came to the edge of the corn fields, again two of the Beni Sakhr sprang up seemingly out of the ground and came riding towards us. Exactly the same interview took place as before and they retired in disgust. We got in at 5, quite delighted with our day. Don't think I have ever spent such a wonderful day.

*Sunday 25:* I'm going on to Petra! What with giving out that I'm a German (for they are desperately afraid of the English), I have got permission and a soldier from the governor and this is always difficult and often impossible, and I can't but think that the finger of Providence points southwards!

*Thursday 29:* Wady Mousa – at length we have arrived and it is worth all the long long way. We descended to the village of Wady Mousa … rode on and soon got into the entrance of the defile which leads to Petra. The Bab es Sik is a passage about half a mile long and in places not more than eight feet wide; the rocks rise on either side straight up 100 feet or so, are sandstone of the most exquisite red and sometimes almost arch overhead. The stream runs between filling all the path, though it used to flow through conduits and the road was paved; oleanders grew along the stream and here and there a sheaf of ivy hung down over the red rock. We went on in ecstasies until suddenly between the narrow opening of the rocks, we saw the most beautiful sight I have ever seen. Imagine a temple cut out of the solid rock, the charming façade supported on great Corinthian columns standing clear, soaring upwards to the very top of the cliff in the most exquisite proportions and carved with groups of figures almost all as fresh as when the chisel left them – all this in the rose red rock, with the sun just touching it and making it look almost transparent. As we went on the gorge widened, on either side the cliffs were cut out into rock tombs of every shape and adorned in every manner, some standing, columned, in the rock, some clear with a pointed roof, some elaborate, some simple, some capped with pointed pyramids, many adorned with a curious form of stair high up over the doorway….The wide gorge opened and brought us out into a kind of square between the cliffs with a rude cut theatre in it and tombs on every side. We went on and got into a great open place the cliffs widening out far on every side and leaving this kind of amphitheatre strewn over with mounds of ruins. And here we camped under a row of the most elaborate tombs, three storeys of pillars and cornices and the whole topped by a great funeral urn. They are extremely rococo, just like the kind of thing you see in a Venetian church above a seventeenth-century doge leaning on his elbow, but time has worn them and weather has stained the rock with exquisite colours….It is like a fairy-tale city, all pink and wonderful. The great paved roads stretch up to a ruined arch and vanish; a solid wall springs up some six feet. 'A rose red city half as old as Time'….

*Friday 30:* I have had a busy day. An hour before dawn Ayoub and I started off riding, with a shepherd to guide us, to the top of Mount Hor … we rode up nearly to the top and then dismounted and climbed to the highest summit on which stands, whose tomb do you think! Aaron's! I have never seen anything like these gorges; the cliffs rise for 1000 feet on either side into the most incredible shapes and coloured! – red, yellow, blue, white, great patterns over them more lovely than any mosaic. I came back to my tents and found we had bought fifty eggs, some figs and a sheep! but unfortunately the sheep has grown rather old in his long journey to us.

*Saturday 31:* We left Petra at 7 this morning with great regret. It was looking exquisite and I longed for another day….

# CAROLINE OF BRUNSWICK

## ◄ 1768–1821 ►

*Caroline of Brunswick, c. 1820 (portrait by J. Lonsdale)*

*Caroline Amelia Elizabeth was born on 17 May 1768, the second daughter of the Duke of Brunswick-Wolfenbüttel, and in 1795 married the Prince of Wales. Bride and groom took an immediate dislike to each other and, although she bore him a daughter, Charlotte, in 1796, they soon formally separated. Her scandalous behaviour led her to be excluded from Court and barred the company of her daughter, so in 1814 Caroline decided to set sail for the continent. After spending some time at Lake Como, she travelled to Tunis, Malta, Athens and Jerusalem, where she made a theatrical entry into the city: 'on horseback, accompanied by a ragtag-and-bobtail suite'. An account of these travels was written by one of her suite and published in 1821. Her behaviour was apparently so outrageous on this long journey that, in 1818, the Regent appointed a commission to collect evidence for a divorce. When he came to the throne in 1820, she was offered an annuity of £50,000 to renounce the title of queen and to continue living abroad; but when she refused and made a triumphal entry into London, the government instituted proceedings against her for adultery. The Divorce Bill was eventually dropped, but she was barred from the Coronation on 19 July 1821 – an act which was called her death-blow. She was taken ill a few days later and died on 7 August.*

*Nazareth*

Our paths, for roads they may not be called, lay during this night principally ascending, until we entered a narrow defile between the hills. This, suddenly opening towards our right, presented us with a view of the small town, or village of Nazareth, situated upon the side of a barren rocky elevation, facing the east, and commanding a long valley. This place appears to suffer much from tyrannical government. Its inhabitants, unable to sustain the burdens imposed upon them, continually emigrate to other territories. The town was in the most wretched state of indigence and misery; the soil around might bid defiance to agriculture; and to the prospect of starvation were frequently added the horrors of the plague. In the valley appeared one of those fountains which, from time immemorial, have been the halting-place of caravans, and sometimes the scene of contention and bloodshed. The women of Nazareth were passing to and from the town, with pitchers upon their heads. We stopped to view the group of camels, with their drivers, who were there reposing; and, calling to mind the manners of the most remote ages, we renewed the solicitations of Abraham's servant unto Rebecca, by the well of Nahor. In the writings of early pilgrims and travellers, this spring is denominated 'The fountain of the Virgin Mary'; and certainly, if there be a spot, throughout the Holy Land, that was undoubtedly honoured by her presence, we may consider this to have been the place; because the situation of a copious spring is not liable to change; and because the custom of repairing thither to draw water has been continued, among the female inhabitants of Nazareth, from the earliest period of its history.

After leaving this fountain, we ascended to the town, and were conducted to the house of the principal Christian inhabitant of Nazareth, where, in the midst of poverty, was more sumptuous fare than is often found in wealthier cities; the convent had largely contributed; but we had reason to fear that many poor families had been pinched to supply our board. All we could do, therefore, as it was brought out with cheerfulness, was to receive it thankfully; and Her Majesty took especial care that those from whom we obtained it should not go unrewarded....

The convent of Nazareth, situated in the lower part of the village, contains about fourteen friars, of the Franciscan order. Its church (erected, as they relate, over the cave in which the Virgin Mary is supposed to have resided) is a handsome edifice; but it is degraded, as a sanctuary, by absurdities too contemptible for notice, if the description of them did not offer an instructive lesson, by showing the abject state to which the human mind may be reduced by superstition. Persons infected with the plague seek a miraculous cure, by rubbing their bodies with the hangings of the sanctuary, and thus communicate infection to the whole town; because, all who enter, salute these hangings with their lips. Many of those unhappy patients believed themselves to be secure, from the moment when they were brought within the walls of this building, although in the last stage of the disorder. As we passed towards the church, one of the friars pointed to some invalids who had recently exhibited marks of the infection: these men were then sitting upon the bare earth, in cells, around the courtyard of the convent, waiting for a miraculous recovery.

Having entered the church, the friars put burning wax tapers into our hands; and, charging us on no account to touch anything, led the way, muttering their prayers. We descended, by a flight of steps, into the cave ... entering, by means of a small door, behind an altar laden with pictures, wax candles and all sorts of superstitious trumpery. They pointed out to us what they called the kitchen and the fireplace of the Virgin Mary. As all these sanctified places, in the Holy Land, contain some supposed miracle for exhibition, the monks of Nazareth have taken care not to be without their share, in supernatural rarities; accordingly, the first thing they show to strangers who descend into this cave, are two stone pillars in the front of it; one of which, separated from its base, is said to sustain its capital and a part of its shaft miraculously in the air, whereas the fact is, that the capital and a piece of the shaft have been fastened on to the roof of the cave; and so clumsily is the rest of the hocus pocus contrived, that what is shown for the lower fragment of the same pillar resting upon the earth, is not of the same substance, the shaft being of granite, the lower portion of marble! The reputation of the broken pillar for healing every kind of disease prevails all over Galilee.

It is from extravagancies of this kind, throughout this country, that devout, but weak men, unable to discriminate between mummery and simple truth, have considered the whole series of evidence to be found there as a tissue of imposture, and have left the Holy Land worse Christians than they were when they arrived....

## Jericho and the Dead Sea

On the 15th Her Majesty departed for Jericho. The road being very perilous from banditti, the Bey furnished Her Majesty an escort of 200 soldiers, of whom the chief, as we were afterwards informed, had been condemned to death a year before, as the chief of a band of robbers. If we had cause of alarm, it was therefore from our trusty chief himself and the soldiers by whom we were surrounded. They certainly had but little of military appearance, but more the air of fugitives from the galleys. One was armed with a gun, another a club, another a bar of iron, and a fourth a sort of fork as a weapon. Neither was their dress more uniform, and themselves exactly the colour of the chestnut. On their head they wore a small and dirty turban, and the rest of their dress was equally unseemly. Such were the men under whose protection, in profound darkness, we accomplished this journey in the deserts of Palestine; in the midst of frightful precipices, and on a road, known by us to be infested with robbers, and on which no dwelling was visible. Notwithstanding all this, Her Majesty's firmness did not appear to be for a moment shaken; nor, such is the importance of example, was it till they were past that we reflected on the perils to which we had been exposed.

In our way hither, having entered a narrow valley, we followed the bed of a torrent, which, after several windings, leads to Mount Adomim: this is a reddish and argillaceous hill, uncultivated like the ground we had hitherto trodden, and having on its summit the ruins of a monastery, or, perhaps, of a khan. After having halted for half an hour, we entered ravines, almost impassable, which appeared to be the effects of a recent convulsion of nature. White mountains, which could not be more aptly compared than to the solfatara of Naples, were to be seen furrowed by fire, and marked with the stains of sulphur. After having descended into frightful abysses, we were obliged to climb up sharp rocks, to procure a sight of the plain of Jericho, which we shortly after reached.

Jericho is at present nothing more than an assemblage of huts built of earth and reeds, covered over with a species of dried fern. Where its celebrated walls once stood, fagots of briers and thistles now scarcely suffice to defend the flocks against the frequent attacks of wild beasts. The Aga inhabits a square tower, in so ruinous a condition that we found considerable difficulty in ascending to the apartment in which he was lodged. This chief of the spahis selected for our night's lodging the most convenient place he could find; for we could not endure the filth and bad smells of the habitation in which our caravan was assembled. Our people took their stations around a large fire in the open air....

The women of Jericho are dressed in a blue chemise, fastened by a girdle; their head is

*General view of Nazareth, by David Roberts*

covered by a veil. Their legs and feet are naked, as are likewise their arms, which are ornamented with bracelets of silver, pewter or glass. They are for the greater part tall and slender; but their forms are usually shrunken; and among the youngest may be noticed a constant struggle between beauty and wretchedness.

The Aga of Jericho added to our escort a few of his people. We crossed a sandy plain, on which were to be seen, at distant intervals, a few prickly shrubs, and a few plants breathing the most delicate perfume. Several authors think that the crown of thorns of Christ was formed of a branch of the rhamnus, a shrub named by the Arabs alausegi, and which is found in great abundance near the Jordan: several volumes have been written either to attack or defend this supposition. Its banks are frequently covered by locusts; the Arabs cook them with great care and find their flavour excellent; but we were not tempted to taste this dish. Where, alas! are the gardens which once covered these banks? Jericho is left without flowers and without harvests.

Our party now drew up in a regular line of march, a few of our men forming the advance guard. The Aga had received notice that a band of Bedouin Arabs had been seen on the preceding evening, and were to pitch their tents for the night on the opposite bank of the Jordan. Lances were perceived behind a rising ground, and horsemen fleeing in several directions; a part of our escort set off at full speed in pursuit of them.

The banks of the sacred river are lofty and covered with trees: its water is yellowish, turbid and of some depth; its breadth is about eighty feet. Charmed with the soft murmurs of the water, to which our ears had been unaccustomed, we joyfully performed the duties of the traveller by ablutions, and brought away several flasks of the holy water we had found so much pleasure in drinking. Our horses experienced some difficulty in crossing the sandy plain which leads to the Dead Sea; our janissaries and Arabs sung, and discharged their pistols; the chief of the escort, mounted on a superb Arabian horse, was the most dexterous; and we followed the example of our guides. We sometimes paced silently, plunged in reverie, the subject of each of which was no doubt different; and at others, giving the reins to our horses, galloped over these sandy plains, breathing perfumes and enjoying our independence. In this way we reached the banks of the Dead Sea.

It is said that this sea, or lake, is twenty leagues in length, and about ten leagues in breadth at the widest part. The Arabs formerly tendered their services to travellers, to conduct them to a pillar coated with bitumen, which they showed as the pillar of salt; but it is impossible at present to penetrate so far without danger, the Bedouins in the vicinity being in a state of constant warfare with travellers....

The water of the Dead Sea is troubled, pungent and bitter. It throws up on its banks pieces of petrified wood and porous stones in a calcined state. In speaking of it, which they do with the most religious respect, many mysterious things are related by the Arabs concerning it.

We afterwards followed, by the mountains, the route leading to the monastery of Saint Sabas. And, never surely was there any sight so dismal and sombre as that of the deep valleys, which are suddenly shut in by a high mountain, perfectly white and easily to be mistaken, at the decline of day, for an enormous spectre whose office it is to defend the passage: the clefts and caverns represent his features, and the ravines supply the folds of his frightful robe. Mountains of ashes, cones mutilated and thrown down, broken rocks of a capricious and fantastic form: such were the objects which met the view for the extent of several leagues, until we came to a more elevated point. This afforded us another sight of the Dead Sea, just as the sun was setting over Arabia Deserta, behind the mountains of Edom.

From this elevation the Dead Sea appeared like a table of lapis lazuli, the golden margin of which was formed by the surrounding mountains.

Still further, the piled rocks resembled, now a fortified city, the walls and buildings of which menaced the starry firmament; and now an amphitheatre having for its spectators and performers kites and vultures; while eagles soared majestically in the air, over their proud domain.

# JAMES SILK BUCKINGHAM

## 1786–1855

*James Silk Buckingham and his wife in oriental dress*

*James Silk Buckingham was born near Falmouth on 25 August 1786. He went to sea at the age of ten and spent several months as a prisoner of war of the French. He finally settled in India and, working with the merchant community, tried to persuade the Egyptian ruler to trade with the British in India via the Red Sea, having investigated this route by learning Arabic and disguising himself as an Egyptian peasant. In 1816 he explored Palestine and Mesopotamia, and the account of his adventures,* Travels in Palestine through the Countries of Basham and Gilead *(1821), went further than anyone so far in debunking the Holy City. In 1825 a second book about his* Travels among the Arab Tribes … *was published. From 1832 to 1837 he was MP for Sheffield and took an especial interest in social reform. Afterwards he became well-known as a lecturer, wrote a number of pamphlets and was at work on his autobiography when he died after a long illness in 1855.*

*The Convent of the Terra Santa*
*January 1816*

As the sun was hastening fast to decline, we quickened the pace of our weary mules, and riding for about half an hour over the rugged face of this mountain's top, we came at five in sight of Jerusalem, on the western brow of this hill, and now but a little below us.

The appearance of this celebrated city, independently of the feelings and recollections which the approach to it cannot fail to awaken, was greatly inferior to my expectations, and had certainly nothing of grandeur or beauty, of stateliness or magnificence about it. It appeared like a walled town of the third or fourth class, having neither towers, nor domes, nor minarets within it, in sufficient numbers to give even a character to its impressions on the beholder; but showing chiefly large flat-roofed buildings, of the most unornamented kind, seated amid rugged hills, on a stoney and forbidding soil, with scarcely a picturesque object in the whole compass of the surrounding view.

We hastened to the gate, which was in the act of closing as we entered it; and turning to the left, and passing through some narrow paved streets, which were unusually clean, we arrived by a circuitous route, at the Latin convent of the Terra Santa....

On being shown up to the friars, I could not help observing that suspicion seemed to exist among them all of my being a poor man; my scanty baggage was eyed with contempt, and twenty questions were asked me in a breath. Fortunately, the kind superior of Nazareth had given me a letter for the procuratore generale here, but as it was some time before this could be got at, I was kept waiting the whole of the time in the gallery....

All was instantly changed [when the letter was produced]: the President of Nazareth, I know not why, having warmly recommended me to his holy care and protection, as a 'Milord Inglese, richissimo, affabilissimo, ed anche doitissimo', messengers were sent out to escort me into the hall of reception, where I met a hearty welcome from four or five of the heads of the church in a circular dome-built library. Sweetmeats and cordials were served; I was hailed as 'ben venuto' by every voice; and, shabby as my appearance was, the respect which was paid to me could not have been exceeded, even to a prince....

Instead of the comfort, apparent equality and cheerfulness, which reigned at Nazareth, and even at Ramlah, all [the friars] seemed here to stand in fear of each other; gloom and jealousy reigned throughout, and the names of the padre superiore and of the procuratore generale were as much dreaded as they were respected.

When we talked of the nature of their duties here, everyone complained of them as severe in the extreme. The tinkle of the bell for service was heard at almost every hour of the day; and, besides getting up two hours before sunrise to celebrate a mass, they were obliged to leave their beds every night at half-past eleven, for midnight prayers. Nothing was talked of but suffering and the difficulty of obedience, ardent desires to return to Europe and a wish to be sent anywhere, indeed, on the out-stations, rather than to continue at Jerusalem.

Not even in a solitary instance did I hear a word of resignation, or of the joy of suffering for Christ's sake, or the love of persecution, or of the paradise found in a life of mortification, so often attributed to these men. Either they must think and feel differently in different societies, or be hypocrites in their behaviour and professions; or else those who have reported such things of them must have drawn a picture widely different from the truth.

For myself, I believe the friars to be, in general, sincere, to display that sincerity whenever they may dare to do so. I am persuaded that they themselves have faith in all the legends which they retail, and that they think their life to be a meritorious one; but as they are still men, they feel sensibly the privations to which they are subject; and all, as far as I could discover, longed escape from them.

One complained, 'I came here for three years only, and have been kept seven; God grant that I may be able to return home at the coming spring.' Another said, 'What can we do? We are poor; the voyage is long; and unless we have permission, and some provision made for our way, how can we think of going?' A third added, 'In Christendom we can amuse ourselves by occasional visits to friends; and, during long fasts, good fish, excellent fruit and exquisite wines are to be had.' While a fourth continued, 'And if one should be taken sick here, either of the plague or any other disease, we have no doctor but an old frate of the convent, no aid but from a few spurious medicines, and nothing, in short, to preserve one's life, dearer than all beside; so that we must end our days unpitied and quit the world before our time.'

These were almost the literal expressions that escaped from the mouths of my visitors, and that too without a question framed to excite them on my part. They were such as I really did not expect to hear....

This being the headquarters and the court of the church-militant on earth, favour and intrigue, no doubt, prevail, and interest becomes necessary to procure the appointments to more agreeable stations, where the duties are less severe, and where the liberty of action is greater.

During my stay at Nazareth, I remember to have met three young friars, one from Damascus, and two from Aleppo, both of them having been ordered there to await their destination from the procuratore generale of Jerusalem. Observing to one of them, who seemed amiable and communicative, that I should be delighted to find his appointment for the Holy City arrive during my stay, so that I might have the pleasure of his company on my way thus far, he replied, 'We are all in doubt as to our destinations, but God grant that mine may be for Aleppo'; 'And mine also,' said another; while the third replied, that 'bad as Damascus was for Christians, he would rather remain ten years there than be condemned to pass five in Jerusalem.' I could not then understand the motive of the dislike to the Holy City, and I was unwilling to give offence by asking an explanation; but now it seemed more intelligible to me.

After the picture of Chateaubriand's first descent at Jaffa, where he found a Spanish friar, with a 'cuore limpido e bianco', who assured him that the life he had led for the last fifty years in the Holy Land was 'un vero paradiso', I knew not what to think of the confessions which I had this evening heard with my own ear. The zeal of this enthusiastic writer may have carried him very far, but surely not to state a deliberate falsehood, so that the conclusion at which I could arrive was, that either the characters of the men or the manner in which they lived had changed, or that such happy individuals as Padre Franciscos Munos were extremely rare.

*The Brothel of the Catholic Monks, Jerusalem*
*22 January 1816*

...Passing in our way through a dark passage, under an arched gate, we observed a large court above, on the stairs of which were several good-looking females, who seemed to invite us up to join them. Accordingly, turning back, we all ascended and were treated with a familiarity which we did not well comprehend, until it was told us that this house had been left as a legacy by some pious Christian to the friars of our convent, and that they suffered it to be occupied rent-free by families, on very improper conditions. This being

*Jerusalem, from the road leading to Bethany, by David Roberts*

told us by a Copt, we conceived it to be a scandal, on account of a difference in their faith; but it was confirmed to us … and we returned to our quarters surprised at the disclosure….

*25 January:* We were by this time close to the Holy Sepulchre, which had not been opened for several days, so that I had yet possessed no opportunity of entering it. Having intimated to our guide all that I had heard of the female establishment of the friars here, which was now close by, he at first denied the fact of its being of the nature represented: by persisting, however, in the accuracy of my information, he at length relented into an admission of its possibility; and by the further influence of three piastres secretly put into his hand, he winked assent, and whispered to me that if I was desirous of it, he would conduct me thither. It was now near the evening, and my wish to get at the truth of this singular state of society determined me to pursue this matter somewhat further: we accordingly went to the house, and while Gabriel, for that was my guardian angel's name, remained in the court below, I ascended the flight of winding stairs which led from the dark street to an open upper court, and from thence again went by another flight to the gallery above, from which the private chambers led off. I was met by an elderly man, of about fifty, who addressed me in Arabic, and I answered him that I was the English traveller, who, but a few days since, had called in company with my companion as we came from the Coptic convent. A door was instantly opened, and I was shown into a room where were mattresses and cushions on the floor, and some little children playing. Presently afterwards there appeared a woman of about thirty, the mother of these children, and the wife of the man who first received me; and who, having named her to me as 'Sitte Tereza', retired. The children were also removed on various pretences made to them; the door was closed, and we were perfectly alone.

All at once, a loud knocking interrupted the scene: the cunning Tereza exclaimed, 'Min hoo?' (who is there?) and, placing her fingers on her lips, implied an injunction of silence. No reply was made; but a second knocking occasioned the door to be opened, and behold my Abyssinian friend, Moosa, appeared, stuttering with rage and scarcely able to contain his anger. I begged him to sit down. Tereza was still more polite and said, 'My dear Sir, won't you take a glass of rakhee, or a pipe, or coffee?' The man replied, surlily, that he could not stay, insisted that he wanted me on urgent business, and declared that he would not stir from the door without taking me with him. I rose and followed him, when he chid me for the folly of the risk that I had exposed myself to. It appeared that, passing by below, he had seen Gabrielli at the door, and suspected me to be within; though this fellow insisted that he knew nothing of the man for whom he enquired.

Moosa, according to his own account, had come up to rescue me from the threatening danger. He then assured me that the system here, to all who were not members of the convent to which the house belonged, was to detain the stranger in the room as long as possible; and that, in the meantime, the husband, or the brother, or some male friend concerned, personated a Turkish soldier by a change of dress and, pretending to have discovered a Christian violating the law, insisted upon the immediate payment of a large sum, or a watch, or some other equivalent, to bribe him to silence; so that the adventurer was sure of being fleeced of all he might possess about his person and be drawn in, perhaps, for promises of more to purchase his escape, while the courtesan and her colleagues divided the spoil.

I had heard before of similar things being done by Turks in Constantinople, but could scarcely credit its existence here, under the circumstances related. Moosa insisted on the fact, and Gabrielli did not pretend to deny it, though he gave no active assent; for dissatisfaction at discovery had made him silent. What I myself witnessed, however, I have faithfully related; and what I myself heard I too firmly believed.

# FRANÇOIS-RENÉ DE CHATEAUBRIAND

## ━━ 1768–1848 ━━

*François-René de Chateaubriand*

*François-René de Chateaubriand was born in St Malo of a noble Breton family. He served for a short time as an ensign and then sailed to North America in 1791, where he spent eight months in the travels recounted in his* Voyage en Amérique. *The Revolution drove him from France and, from 1793 to 1800, he lived in England. His first major book,* Essai sur les révolutions, *appeared in 1797, and the enthusiastic reception his tragic love stories,* Atala *(1801) and* René *(1805), received established his reputation as one of the leading figures of early French Romanticism. His* Génie du christianisme *(1802) raised him to the foremost position amongst the men of letters of his day. In 1803 he was appointed secretary to the embassy in Rome, but, refusing to serve under Napoleon, he set out for the East in 1806. He travelled for a year and the account of his journey,* Itinéraire de Paris à Jérusalem, *went into twelve editions. Soon after his visit, the Church of the Holy Sepulchre burnt down and he thus became 'the last traveller by whom it was visited, and for the same reason I shall be its last historian'. From 1814 to 1830 he followed the career of a statesman and then devoted his old age to the completion of his memoirs, which were published posthumously in 1848.*

*First View of the River Jordan*

I passed two whole hours (October 5th) in strolling on the banks of the Dead Sea in spite of my Bethlehemites who urged me to leave this dangerous country. I was desirous of seeing the Jordan at the place where it discharges itself into the lake; an essential point which Hasselquist alone has hitherto explored; but the Arabs refused to conduct me to it, because the river near its mouth turns off to the left and approaches the mountains of Arabia. I was therefore obliged to make up my mind to proceed to the curve of the river that was nearest to us. We broke up our camp and advanced for an hour and a half with excessive difficulty over a fine white sand. We were approaching a grove of balm trees and tamarinds, which to my great astonishment I perceived in the midst of this sterile tract. The Arabs all at once stopped and pointed to something that I had not yet remarked at the bottom of a ravine. Unable to make out what it was, I perceived what appeared to be sand in motion. On drawing nearer to this singular object, I beheld a yellow current, which I could scarcely distinguish from the sands on its shores. It was deeply sunk below its banks, and its sluggish stream rolled slowly on. This was the Jordan.

I had surveyed the great rivers of America with that pleasure which solitude and nature impart; I had visited the Tiber with enthusiasm, and sought with the same interest the Eurotas and the Cephisus; but I cannot express what I felt at the sight of the Jordan. Not only did this river remind me of a renowned antiquity, and one of the most celebrated names that the most exquisite poetry ever confided to the memory of man; but its shores likewise presented to my view the theatre of the miracles of my religion. Judea is the only country in the world that revives in the traveller the memory of human affairs and of celestial things, and which, by this combination, produces in the soul a feeling and ideas which no other religion is capable of exciting.

The Arabs stripped and plunged into the Jordan. I durst not follow their example on account of the fever by which I was still tormented; but I fell upon my knees on the bank with my two servants and the dragoman of the monastery. Having forgotten to bring a Bible, we could not repeat the passages of Scripture relating to the spot where we now were; but the dragoman, who knew the customs of the place, began to sing: Ave maris stella. We responded like sailors at the end of their voyage....I then took up some water from the river in a leather vessel: it did not seem to me as sweet as sugar, according to the expression of a pious missionary. I thought it, on the contrary, rather brackish; but though I drank a considerable quantity, I felt no inconvenience from it: nay, I even think it would be very pleasant if it were purified from the sand which it carries along with it....

*The Arabs*

The Arabs, wherever I have seen them, in Judea, in Egypt and even in Barbary, have appeared to me to be rather tall than short. Their demeanour is haughty. They are well made and active. They have an oval head, the brow high and arched, aquiline nose, large eyes with a watery and uncommonly gentle look. Nothing about them would proclaim the savage, if their mouths were always shut; but as soon as they begin to speak, you hear a harsh and strongly aspirated language, and perceive long and beautifully white teeth – like those of jackals and ounces: differing in this respect from the American savage, whose ferocity is in his looks, and human expression in his mouth.

The Arab women are still taller in proportion than the men. Their carriage is dignified; and by the regularity of their features, the beauty of their figures, and the disposition of their veils, they somewhat remind you of the statues of the priestesses and of the Muses. This must, however, be understood with some restriction: these beautiful statues are often clothed in rags; a wretched, squalid and suffering look degrade those forms so elegant; a copper teint conceals the regularity of the features; in a word, to behold these women as I have just delineated them, you must view them at a distance, confine yourself to the general appearance and not enter into particulars....

All that has been related concerning the passion of the Arabs for stories is true, and of this I shall give one example. In the night that we passed on the shore of the Dead Sea, our Bethlehemites were seated round their fire, their pieces being laid on the ground by their sides; while their horses, tied to stakes, formed a second circle about them. Having drunk their coffee and talked a good deal together, these Arabs all became silent, with the exception of their sheikh. By the light of the fire I could see his expressive gestures, his black beard, his white teeth, the various forms which he gave to his garments in the course of his relation. His companions listened with profound attention, all bending forward with their faces over the fire, sometimes ejaculating an expression of admiration, at others, repeating, with emphasis, the gestures of the narrator. Some horses' heads advancing over the company and discernible in the shade, contributed to give this scene the most picturesque character, especially if we include in the view a corner of the Dead Sea and the mountains of Judea.

If I had studied with such interest the American hordes on the banks of their lakes, what a different species did I here contemplate! I had before me the descendants of the primitive race of mankind; I beheld them with the same manners which they have retained ever since the days of Hagar and Ishmael; I beheld them in the same desert that was assigned to them by God for their inheritance....

What particularly distinguishes the Arabs from the tribes of the New World is, that amidst the rudeness of the former, you still perceive a certain degree of delicacy in their manners; you perceive that they are natives of that East which is the cradle of all the arts, all the sciences and all religions. Buried at the extremity of the West, in a by-corner of the universe, the Canadian inhabits valleys shaded by eternal forests and watered by immense rivers: the Arab, cast as it were, upon the high road of the world, between Africa and Asia, roves in the brilliant regions of Aurora over a soil without trees and without water. Among the tribes descended from Ishmael, it is requisite that there should be masters and servants, domestic animals, and a liberty in subjection to laws. Among the American hordes man still enjoys in unsocial solitude his proud and cruel independence....He is not connected by his origin with the great civilized nations; the names of his ancestors are not to be found in the annals of empires; the contemporaries of his ancestors are ancient oaks that are still standing. Monuments of nature and not of history, the tombs of his fathers rise unheeded among unknown forests. In a word, with the American everything proclaims the savage, who has not yet arrived at a state of civilization; in the Arab, everything indicates the civilized man who has returned to the savage state.

*The Church of the Holy Sepulchre*

It is obvious, in the first place, that the Church of the Holy Sepulchre is composed of three churches: that of the Holy Sepulchre, properly so called; that of Calvary; and the church of the Discovery of the Cross.

The first is built in the valley at the foot of Calvary, on the spot where it is known that the body of Christ was deposited. This church is in the form of the cross, the chapel of the Holy Sepulchre constituting in fact the nave of the edifice. It is circular, like the Pantheon

*First sight of the River Jordan (photo by James Graham, c. 1853)*

at Rome, and is lighted only by a dome, beneath which is the sepulchre. Sixteen marble columns adorn the circumference of this rotunda: they are connected by seventeen arches and support an upper gallery, likewise composed of sixteen columns and seventeen arches, of smaller dimensions than those of the lower range. Niches corresponding with the arches appear above the frieze of the second gallery, and the dome springs from the arch of these niches. The latter were formerly decorated with mosaics, representing the twelve apostles, St Helena, the emperor Constantine, and three other portraits unknown.

The choir of the church of the Holy Sepulchre is to the east of the nave of the tomb: it is double, as in the ancient cathedrals; that is to say, it has first a place with stalls for the priests, and beyond that a sanctuary raised two steps above it. Round this double sanctuary run the aisles of the choir, and in these aisles are situated the chapels....

It is likewise in the aisle on the right, behind the choir, that we find the two flights of steps leading, the one to the church of Calvary, the other to the church of the Discovery of the Holy Cross. The first ascends to the top of Calvary, the second conducts you down underneath it: for the Cross was erected on the summit of Golgotha and found again under that hill....

The architecture of the church is evidently of the age of Constantine: the Corinthian order prevails throughout. The columns are either too heavy or too slender, and their diameter is almost always disproportionate to their height. Some double columns which support the frieze of the choir are, however, in a very good style. The church being lofty and spacious, the profile of the cornices displays a considerable degree of grandeur; but as the arches which separate the choir from the nave were stopped up about sixty years ago, the 'horizontal line is broken, and you no longer enjoy a view of the whole of the vaulted roof.

The church has no vestibule, nor any other entrance than two side doors, only one of which is ever opened. Thus this structure appears to have never had any exterior decoration. It is besides concealed by shabby buildings, and by the Greek convents erected close to its walls.

The small structure of marble which covers the Holy Sepulchre is in the figure of a canopy, adorned with semi-gothic arches; it rises with elegance under the dome, by which it receives light, but it is spoiled by a massive chapel which the Armenians have obtained permission to erect at one end of it. The interior of this canopy presents to the view a very plain tomb of white marble, which adjoins on one side to the wall of the monument, and serves the Catholic religious for an altar. This is the tomb of Jesus Christ....

Christian readers will perhaps enquire what were my feelings on entering this awful place. I really cannot tell. So many reflections rushed at once upon my mind, that I was unable to dwell upon any particular idea. I continued near half an hour upon my knees in the little chamber of the Holy Sepulchre, with my eyes rivetted on the stone, from which I had not the power to turn them....

We visited all the stations till we came to the summit of Calvary. Where shall we look in antiquity for anything so impressive, so wonderful, as these last scenes described by the Evangelists?...I had just beheld the monuments of Greece, and my mind was still profoundly impressed with their grandeur; but how far inferior were the sensations which they excited to those which I felt at the sight of the places commemorated in the Gospel!

I did not leave the sacred structure without stopping at the monuments of Godfrey and Baldwin. They face the entrance of the church and stand against the wall of the choir. I saluted the ashes of these royal chevaliers, who were worthy of reposing near the tomb which they had rescued. These ashes are those of Frenchmen, and they are the only mortal remains interred beneath the shadow of the tomb of Christ. What an honorable distinction for my country!

# ROBERT CURZON
## ◄━━ 1810–73 ━━►

*Robert Curzon, c.1840 (study by Richard Beard)*

*Robert Curzon was the son of Harriett Anne, Baroness de la Zouche, whose title he was to inherit. Born in London on 16 March 1810, he was educated at Charterhouse and Christ Church, Oxford. He left university without a degree in 1831 when he was returned to Parliament as a member for Clitheroe, but was disenfranchised the following year as a result of the Reform Bill. Almost immediately he set out on a Grand Tour and travelled throughout Egypt, Syria, Turkey and Greece during 1833–4, searching for ancient manuscripts in monastery libraries. Whilst in Jerusalem he witnessed the mass asphyxiation of over 500 people during the ceremony of the Sacred Fire, which is so vividly described in the following extract from his subsequent book, Visits to Monasteries in the Levant, published in 1849. He was back in Egypt in 1837–8 visiting the Coptic monasteries of the Wadi Natron, south of Alexandria. In 1841 he returned to the Bosphorus as Lord Stratford de Redcliffe's private secretary and two years later became a joint commissioner on the Anglo-Russian Commission to define the frontier between Turkey and Persia. This led to his second book, Armenia: A Year at Erzeroom, which went into three editions in 1854. After being taken ill, he returned to England and spent the rest of his life in Sussex, where he died on 2 August 1873.*

It was on Friday, the 3rd of May (Good Friday, according to the calendar of the Greeks), that my companions and myself went, about five o'clock in the evening, to the Church of the Holy Sepulchre, where we had places assigned us in the gallery, of the Latin monks, as well as a good bedroom in their convent. The church was very full, and the numbers kept increasing every moment. We first saw a small procession of the Copts go round the sepulchre, and after them one of the Syrian Maronites. I then went to bed and at midnight was awakened to see the procession of the Greeks, which was rather grand. By the rules of their church they are not permitted to carry any images and therefore to make up for this they bore aloft a piece of brocade, upon which was embroidered a representation of the body of our Saviour. This was placed in the tomb, and, after some short time, brought out again and carried into the chapel of the Greeks, when the ceremonies of the night ended....After the Greek procession I went quietly to bed again and slept soundly till next morning.

The behaviour of the pilgrims was riotous in the extreme; the crowd was so great that many persons actually crawled over the heads of others, and some made pyramids of men by standing on each other's shoulders, as I have seen them do at Astley's. At one time, before the church was so full, they made a race-course round the sepulchre; and some, almost in a state of nudity, danced about with frantic gestures, yelling and screaming as if they were possessed.

Altogether it was a scene of disorder and profanation, which it is impossible to describe. In consequence of the multitude of people and the quantities of lamps, the heat was excessive, and a steam arose which prevented your seeing clearly across the church. But every window and cornice, and every place where a man's foot could rest, excepting the gallery which was reserved for Ibrahim Pasha and ourselves appeared to be crammed with people; for 17,000 pilgrims were said to be in Jerusalem, almost the whole of whom had come to the Holy City for no other reason than to see the sacred fire....

The next morning a way was made through the crowd for Ibrahim Pasha, by the soldiers with the butt-ends of their muskets, and by the kavasses with their kour-batches and whips made by a quantity of small rope. The Pasha sat in the gallery, on a divan which the monks had made for him between the two columns nearest to the Greek chapel. They had got up a sort of procession to do him honour, the appearance of which did not add to the solemnity of the scene: three monks playing crazy fiddles led the way, then came the choristers with lighted candles, next two Nizam soldiers with muskets and fixed bayonets; a number of doctors, instructors and officers, tumbling over each other's heels, brought up the rear: he was received by the women, of whom there were thousands in the church, with a very peculiar shrill cry, which had a strange unearthly effect. It was the mono-syllable la, la, la, uttered in a shrill trembling tone, which I thought much more like pain than rejoicing. The Pasha was dressed in full trousers of dark cloth, a light lilac-coloured jacket, and a red cap without a turban. When he was seated, the monks brought us some sherbet, which was excellently made; and as our seats were very near the great man, we saw everything in an easy and luxurious way; and it being announced that the Mohammedan Pasha was ready, the Christian miracle, which had been waiting for some time, was now on the point of being displayed.

The people were by this time become furious; they were worn out with standing in such a crowd all night, and as the time approached for the exhibition of the holy fire they could not contain themselves for joy. Their excitement increased as the time for the miracle in which all believed drew near. At about one o'clock a magnificent procession moved out of the Greek chapel. It conducted the Patriarch three times round the tomb; after which he took off his outer robes of cloth of silver and went into the sepulchre, the door of which was then closed. The agitation of the pilgrims was now extreme: they screamed aloud; and the dense mass of people shook to and fro, like a field of corn in the wind.

There is a round hole in one part of the chapel over the sepulchre, out of which the holy fire is given, and up to this the man who had agreed to pay the highest sum for this honour was conducted by a strong guard of soldiers. There was silence for a minute; and then a light appeared out of the tomb, and the happy pilgrim received the holy fire from the Patriarch within. It consisted of a bundle of thin wax-candles, lit and enclosed in an iron frame, to prevent their being torn asunder and put out in the crowd; for a furious battle commenced immediately; everyone being so eager to obtain the holy light, that one man put out the candle of his neighbour in trying to light his own. It is said that as much as 10,000 piastres has been paid for the privilege of first receiving the holy fire, which is believed to ensure eternal salvation. The Copts got eight purses this year for the first candle they gave to a pilgrim of their own persuasion.

This was the whole of the ceremony; there was no sermon or prayers, except a little chanting during the processions, and nothing that could tend to remind you of the awful event which this feast was designed to commemorate.

Soon you saw the lights increasing in all directions, everyone having lit his candle from the holy flame the chapels, the galleries and every corner where a candle could possibly be displayed, immediately appeared to be in a blaze. The people in their frenzy put the bunches of lighted tapers to their faces, hands and breasts, to purify themselves from their sins. The Patriarch was carried out of the sepulchre in triumph, on the shoulders of the people he had deceived, amid the cries and exclamations of joy which resounded from every nook of the immense pile of buildings. As he appeared in a fainting state, I supposed that he was ill; but I found that it is the uniform custom on these occasions to feign insensibility, that the pilgrims may imagine he is overcome with the glory of the Almighty, from whose immediate presence they believe him to have returned.

In a short time the smoke of the candles obscured everything in the place, and I could see it rolling in great volumes out at the aperture at the top of the dome. The smell was terrible; and three unhappy people, overcome by heat and bad air, fell from the upper range of galleries and were dashed to pieces on the heads of the people below. One poor Armenian lady, seventeen years of age, died where she sat, of heat, thirst and fatigue.

After a while, when he had seen all that was to be seen, Ibrahim Pasha got up and went away, his numerous guards making a line for him by main force through the dense mass of people which filled the body of the church. As the crowd was so immense, we waited for a little while and then set out all together to return to our convent. I went first and my friends followed me, the soldiers making way for us across the church. I got as far as the place where the Virgin is said to have stood during the Crucifixion, when I saw a number of people lying one on another all about this part of the church, and as far as I could see towards the door. I made my way between them as well as I could, till they were so thick that there was actually a great heap of bodies on which I trod. It then suddenly struck me they were all dead! I had not perceived this at first, for I thought they were only very much fatigued with the ceremonies and had lain down to rest themselves there; but when I came to so great a heap of bodies I looked down at them and saw that sharp, hard appearance of the face which is never to be mistaken. Many of them were quite black with suffocation, and further on were others all bloody and covered with the brains and entrails of those who had been trodden to pieces by the crowd.

At this time there was no crowd in this part of the church; but a little farther on, round

*The Shrine of the Holy Sepulchre, by David Roberts*

the corner towards the great door, the people, who were quite panic-struck, continued to press forward, and everyone was doing his utmost to escape. The guards outside, frightened at the rush from within, thought that the Christians wished to attack them, and the confusion soon grew into a battle. The soldiers with their bayonets killed numbers of fainting wretches, and the walls were spattered with blood and brains of men who had been felled, like oxen, with the butt-ends of the soldiers' muskets. Everyone struggled to defend himself or to get away, and in the mêlée all who fell were immediately trampled to death by the rest. So desperate and savage did the fight become, that even the panic-struck and frightened pilgrims appeared at last to have been more intent upon the destruction of each other than desirous to save themselves.

For my part, as soon as I perceived the danger, I had cried out to my companions to turn back, which they had done; but I myself was carried on by the press till I came near the door, where all were fighting for their lives. Here, seeing certain destruction before me, I made every endeavour to get back. An officer of the Pasha's, who by his star was a colonel or bin bashee, equally alarmed with myself, was also trying to return: he caught hold of my cloak, or bournouse, and pulled me down on the body of an old man who was breathing out his last sigh. As the officer was pressing me to the ground, we wrestled together among the dying and the dead with the energy of despair. I struggled with this man till I pulled him down, and happily got again upon my legs (I afterwards found that he never rose again). I stood up for a minute among the press of people, held up on the uncomfortable footing of dead bodies, by the dense crowd who were squeezed together in this narrow part of the church. We all stood still for a short time, when of a sudden the crowd swayed, a cry arose, the crowd opened, and I found myself standing in the centre of a line of men, with another line opposite to me, all pale and ghastly with torn and bloody clothes, and there we stood glaring at each other; but in a moment a sudden impulse seized upon us, with a shriek that echoed in the long aisles of the Church of the Holy Sepulchre (how terribly desecrated at this moment!), the two adverse lines dashed at each other, and I was soon engaged tearing and wrestling with a thin half-naked man, whose legs were smeared with blood. The crowd again fell back, and by desperate fighting and hard struggles I made my way back into the body of the church, where I found my friends, and we succeeded in reaching the sacristy of the Catholics, and thence the room which had been assigned to us by the monks, but not without a fierce conflict at the door of the sacristy with a crowd of frightened pilgrims, who tried to press through with us. I thanked God for my escape – I had a narrow chance. The dead were lying in heaps, even upon the stone of unction; and I saw full 400 unhappy people, dead and living, heaped promiscuously one upon another, in some places above five feet high....

We stayed in our room two hours before we ventured to make another attempt to escape from this scene of horror; and then walking close together, with all our servants round us, we made a bold push and got out of the door of the church. By this time most of the bodies were removed; but twenty or thirty were still lying in distorted attitudes at the foot of Mount Calvary; and fragments of clothes, turbans, shoes and handkerchiefs, clotted with blood and dirt, were strewed all over the pavement....

In the court in the front of the church the sight was pitiable; mothers weeping over their children – the sons bending over the dead bodies of their fathers; and one poor woman was clinging to the hand of her husband, whose body was fearfully mangled. Most of the sufferers were pilgrims and strangers. The Pasha was greatly moved by this scene of woe; and he again and again commanded his officers to give the poor people every assistance in their power, and very many by his humane efforts were rescued from death.

I was much struck by the sight of two old men with white beards, who had been seeking for each other among the dead; they met as I was passing by, and it was affecting to see them kiss and shake hands, and congratulate each other on having escaped from death.

When the bodies were removed, many were discovered standing upright, quite dead; and near the church door one of the soldiers was found thus standing, with his musket shouldered, among the bodies which reached nearly as high as his head; this was in a corner near the great door on the right side as you come in. It seems that this door had been shut, so that many who stood near it were suffocated in the crowd; and when it was opened the rush was so great, that numbers were thrown down and never rose again, being trampled to death by the press behind them. The whole court before the entrance of the church was covered with bodies laid in rows, by the Pasha's orders, so that their friends might find them and carry them away. As we walked home we saw numbers of people carried out, some dead, some horribly wounded and in a dying state, for they had fought with their heavy silver inkstands and daggers.

In the evening I was not sorry to retire early to rest in the low vaulted room in the strangers' house attached to the monastery of St Salvador. I was weary and depressed after the agitating scenes of the morning, and my lodging was not rendered more cheerful by there being a number of corpses laid out in their shrouds in the stone court beneath its window. It is thought by these superstitious people that a shroud washed in the fountain of Siloam, and blessed at the tomb of our Saviour, forms a complete suit of armour for the body of a sinner deceased in the faith, and that, clad in this invulnerable panoply, he may defy the devil and all his angels. For this reason every pilgrim when journeying has his shroud with him, with all its different parts and bandages complete; and to many they became useful sooner than they expected....

# JAMES FINN
### 1806–72

James Finn

James Finn served as Her Majesty's Consul for Jerusalem and Palestine from 1845 to 1863. A pioneer for the resettlement of the Jews in Eretz Israel, he was a devoted friend of the Jews and often protected them from the Ottoman authorities. At the same time, he was a devoted Christian and engaged in missionary activities – a fact which led many Jews to complain that he was trying to convert them. In assisting the Jews of Jerusalem, he sometimes overlooked the instructions of his own superiors, and it has been suggested that this precipitated the end of his service in Palestine. He wrote several books about the Jews, including The Jews of China (1849) and The Orphan Colony of the Jews of China (1872). After his death in 1872, his widow edited his book, Stirring Times, describing the whole period of his time in Jerusalem. His Byeways in Palestine was also published posthumously in 1877.

*Jerusalem without a Garrison*
*September 1853*

On entering the city, after the parting scene of our battalion [which was withdrawn from Jerusalem by the Turks during its war with Russia – the first time the city had been left undefended since the Crusades], the gates were found to be sentinelled with common Tufenkchies.

We had been well accustomed to the appearance of the Tufenkchies, called out of compliment by foreign consuls the 'municipal police', but in reality ragged hobbledehoys, bearing no other emblem of office than a peeled wand in hand, and chiefly employed in conveying official messages from the Seraglio....

Our new Tufenkchie sentinels were in no way superior to those heretofore seen in Jerusalem; they were, in fact, the very same mean-looking persons, only they were now furnished with old-fashioned rusty guns and were, in the absence of any military, posted at the city gates.

These Tufenkchies for the city, and Bashi-Bozuks (irregular horse) for the country, were our only government defence for the whole province, extending from Jeneen to El-Arish (i.e the north of Samaria to the Egyptian desert), at a time when the peasant factions were rife with turbulence, and the Bedouin hordes had recently approached within sight of our crenellated walls. The men came into the streets and bazaars fully armed as they were. When we had sentinels at the gates in ordinary times they had at least to leave their spears, if not their guns, with the guard before passing into the city....

While the government was thus powerless the peasantry as well as the Bedouin were in full activity. Several armourers in Jerusalem were at work night and day repairing arms. Old feuds were revived, offences long put aside, though not forgotten, were now remembered, and everybody was talking about vengeance and battles and victories over this faction or that....

During the interval in which military protection had no existence for us, irregularities of all kinds naturally took place, such as robbery on the high roads, the revival of the faction feuds of which we have lately had so much, and other acts of petty resistance to government authority on the part of the peasantry. The opportunity was eagerly seized for everybody to do as they liked, though the results might have been worse than they actually were.

In less than a week after the departure of the troops the people of Abu Dees, a village just across the Mount of Olives, to the east, were plundering the shepherds of Malhha, one of the Hhassaniyeh villages to the south of Jerusalem.

Soon afterwards, on a lovely Sunday afternoon, I was at my cottage door at the Talibiyeh (our country place, within a mile west of the city), released from the cares of the past week ... when in one moment a rush of about thirty men of Malhha (peasantry, of course) scaled our low boundary wall, dashing forward, shouting, most of them stripped to the waist, and all armed with guns, pistols and khamnjurs (the short sword in common use among them).

We called out to them, 'Whither away friends?' But they were too eager to stop and explain.

Our first supposition was naturally that they were going to take revenge on the people of Abu Dees, that village being exactly in the line they were taking, although the desperate haste seemed rather unnecessary. It turned out that this was not their present enterprise; the Abu Dees foray had been already dealt with, retaliation made and the flocks recovered, to the number of about 200 head.

The present affair was that the same flocks had again been laid hold of just at the foot of my grounds ... by a roving party of wild Bedouin – Tiyâhah Arabs from the far south....

Never before had we known wild desert plunderers to exercise their vocation under the very walls of Jerusalem. How near the city gates (and now harmless guns) they had actually ventured we soon found out, and also that there were some cattle which, however tempting, even these wild fellows had a wholesome fear of meddling with.

Two of the ladies and children of our party had been attending the afternoon service at Christchurch on Mount Zion, and our groom, an Egyptian and a shrewd old fellow, had gone down the hill with two saddle asses to bring them back, shortly before the alarm of the peasantry. The Bedouin, mounted on their dromedaries, met our groom at the foot of the ascent to the Jaffa gate of the city and cast a longing eye at the led animals, one of which was a remarkably fine specimen of the Egyptian ass, and of course somewhat valuable.

'Whose are those?' asked the Bedouin.

'The English consul's; best for you not so much as to look at them,' retorted our groom. The Bedouin were of his opinion and rode forward, to fall in five minutes afterwards with the flock of sheep and goats and sweep them off by way of comfort at having had to exercise so much self-denial. Fortune was against them here too, for, as we have seen, the peasant owners somehow got wind of what was going on and came to the rescue just in time to decide the Bedouin upon a hasty retreat minus the cattle....

Within the city I found people in a state of alarm on account of burglaries by night, which were becoming a frequent occurrence. So much gunpowder was fired off in order to frighten away real or imaginary robbers that people persuaded themselves that attacks were much more frequent than they really were....

The chief of police was well known to be the head of the burglars. He was notoriously the worst man in the country and had been removed from the office some five years before through the influence of our embassy in Constantinople on account of his concern in the murder of a British subject....

Now however the old chief had once more got himself back into office; and though he was careful not to get into the hands of the consulate, people were very much frightened at the robberies which were committed in the houses of natives and of many Europeans. Times were no doubt very favourable for the burglars, whether village peasants or town thieves, with their allies in the police....

[After more hostilities amongst the local Bedouin in October] a battalion of Turkish troops arrived ... to garrison the city. It consisted of six companies and was commanded by a Bin-Bashi, or major.... Though glad enough to hear of any military occupation of the city, we were nevertheless dissatisfied at this particular corps being destined for us, seeing that it was the one which had disgraced itself by aiding the fanatic massacre of Christians at Aleppo a few years before. This circumstance added new force to the sinister forebodings of the poor native Christians, who had never ceased to expect a sudden rising of the Moslems and a massacre at least as soon as war should be announced. However, we had once more soldiers in the barracks and sentinels at the gates, and it was hoped there would now be some control exercised over the peasantry; that the Bedouin would retire from the mountains into their own deserts....

*The Condition of the Jews in Jerusalem, 1854*

The stagnation of trade, caused by the [Crimean] war and the scarcity caused by the corn supplies being kept back out of the market, caused distress to all classes....

But now special causes were at work and produced so great an amount of distress as we

*Bedouin at the Damascus Gate, Jerusalem, by David Roberts*

had never known before in Jerusalem. The Christian poor were relieved by the communities to which they severally belonged; the great convents opened for their aid some of the stores of grain, always in reserve for time of need. The Moslems, to some extent, aided each other. The laws of hospitality are held so sacred that even a wealthy Moslem, who might be keeping, locked up, a supply of corn which ought to have been available for supply in the open market, and who was thus helping to produce famine among the poor, would scarcely venture to turn from his door a hungry brother who might present himself at supper-time among the guests or among the retainers of the house.

The people for whom alone there were no reserve stores, no helpers, no richer brethren from whose table so much as a crumb might be picked up, were the Jews.

For them there was absolutely no provision in this time of dire distress. Worse still, the fund from which some among them had been in the habit of receiving a pittance, if only a few shillings a year, was now exhausted....

The rain had fallen in January and again at the beginning of February. At various times during this season we have not only snow, but rain in torrents; there is then no more fear of water being scarce for those who have cisterns. The water-supply of Jerusalem is not from springs, but each house has its own cistern, into which the rain is collected as it falls upon the flat roofs and terraces.

But in the Jewish quarter it is always scarce, first, because of the crowded state of the houses, in each of which several families live; secondly, because the Moslem landlords have allowed the cisterns to fall into disrepair, so that the greater number of them hold little or no water. Hence the poor Jews have always to buy water, which they obtain from the peasantry, who bring it into the city in skins on their asses, from the springs of Siloam, Lifta and elsewhere. When the rain has been abundant, the Jews have to pay less; but when the rains are delayed, exorbitant prices are charged, and the misery and suffering endured by men, women and children in the Jewish quarter, for want of water to drink, are grievous to witness.

The state of poverty among the Jews at this time exceeded anything we had before known. Parents were said to be selling their children to Moslems, as the only way of preserving their lives. Some were found dead in their rooms. Among those whom we personally knew there was scarcely a family that was not in the deepest distress....

A small ladies' society was formed for the purpose of raising funds and for visiting the Jewish quarter. The amount of squalid poverty discovered there was truly appalling....

For the most serious part of the matter was this – that the wretchedness was to be found to be anything but temporary – not mere passing distress, caused by the war, by the price of corn, or fuel, or the diminution of funds, but a chronic state of hopeless pauperism – was found to be at all times the condition of the great majority of Jews in the Holy City....

Worst of all they had no employment whereby they might have received, if only bare bread and water. They had never had any employment. There was none for them to have. And yet many of them were artisans, carpenters, tin-smiths, glaziers, dyers, tailors, etc., etc. We knew this because we have always found that it was in the Jewish quarter we could find people able to do for us Europeans such works as the oriental mechanics did not understand, and we knew by experience that the Jews were not only able to work, but that they were thankful and eager to be employed.

But there was no work for them. Oriental Christians have so great a prejudice and superstitious hatred of Jews that they would not on any account have dealings with them. The Moslems had artisans of their own, and even when they needed and employed the superior skill or knowledge of some Jewish workman, it was long before the poor Jew could get the money due to him for his work, and in but too many cases he was too timid to press for payment, and thus never got it at all. Of all the inhabitants of Jerusalem, there were at that period none to employ Jews and pay them for their labour, but the few families belonging to our English congregation....

All this led my wife and myself to make increased exertions for carrying out our long projected design of relieving the Jewish condition of chronic poverty by means of employment of an agricultural character.

A plot of ground of about eight to twelve English acres had been purchased for this object in 1852, on which, as soon as money could be obtained for supplying wages, some of the poor had been set to work....

We were not so sanguine as to expect pallid creatures, weakened by hunger and disease, to perform the labours of healthy robust peasants of the villages, but at least they could clear off the loose stones from the land in baskets; they could assist in building up dry walls of enclosure with the guidance of a few peasants; they could carry water from the cistern, and they could learn to do other things....

It might have been dangerous in those days for weak defenceless Jews to go alone even so far from Jerusalem to work among the native peasantry. But there was no risk in their doing so while the work was known and understood to be under the supervision, although in an informal way, of a consul. One day a peasant, one of the former owners of the ground, gave a little trouble, while the Jews were building the outer wall of enclosure. The peasant endeavoured to interfere and to defraud us a bit of land; he used threatening language and then threw stones. A complaint was made to the pasha, and next morning the offender found himself in prison. After a day or two he came and brought a respectable Moslem of the city as security for his good behaviour. Next day he appeared, humbly begging to be allowed to do some ploughing, which the Jews were not strong enough to do. We found him at work among them – laughing, skipping and running – and there was never another attempt at rough usage of our Jewish workmen.

After operations were fairly started, I one day, after a hard day's office work, rode out towards the plantation to see the men return from labour. They were met coming over the lanes and fields carrying their baskets and tools on their shoulders; a ragged troop, very ragged but very happy, singing a chorus in Hebrew, 'We are labourers in the field of Abraham, our father.'

My eyes filled with tears as the words came to recollection, ' They shall return to Zion with singing, and everlasting joy shall be upon their heads', taking this as a very small indication of the better days to come for their nation....

# WILLIAM HOLMAN HUNT

## ◄ 1827–1910 ►

*William Holman Hunt, 1901 (portrait by W.B. Richmond)*

*William Holman Hunt was born in London on 2 April 1827. He left school at thirteen, but soon began learning art at evening school and, in 1845, was admitted as a student at the Royal Academy. The following year he exhibited his first picture 'Hark!'. Whilst at the RA he met John Millais and Dante Gabriel Rossetti, and in 1848 the three young men laid the foundation of the Pre-Raphaelite Brotherhood, which aimed at detailed and uncompromising truth to nature. The first of his Pre-Raphaelite works was 'Rienzi' (1849). His growing success enabled him to carry out a project which had been forming in his mind for a long time – a visit to the Holy Land in order to paint biblical subjects in their actual surroundings. Leaving England in January 1854 he spent two years in Jerusalem. He soon began 'The Finding of Christ in the Temple' and, encamping on the western shore of the Dead Sea, started work on 'The Scapegoat'. He returned to the Holy Land three more times – in 1869, when he spent two years there painting one of his most characteristic works, 'The Shadow of Death'; in 1875 and again in 1892. In 1905 he was awarded the Order of Merit and also published his Pre-Raphaelitism and the Pre-Raphaelite Brotherhood, a two-volume work which told the story of his life as well as being the best-documented memoir of the movement. He died in London on 7 September 1910.*

*'The Scapegoat'*
The Dead Sea, 1854

While thus detained in Jerusalem news came that the whole of southern Syria was in disorder. The troops being withdrawn, the sheikhs concluded that they could mass their forces and get rid of the hateful Turk. Hebron itself from some cause (perhaps having an Osmanli garrison in the town) elected to hold out for the established power. Thus far the struggle was a political one, but the patriotic effort of the insurgents often degenerated into mere lawlessness and gave encouragement to village desperadoes to embark on felonious enterprises of their own, so that native travellers reported that the roads were quite impracticable. I had no intention of giving up the Scapegoat subject, cost what it might.....

I had brought the goat that had been selected by me several weeks previously to serve as my model on the spot. All the way he was provokingly blatant, he walked and was carried in turns, in either position his object seemed to be to attract attention – the very reverse of our own – doing this whether we were threading our way within earshot of villages either along the bottom of a valley or over the saddle of a hill-pass. We could detect by the wild barkings of dogs that the kid's cry for help was heard, but probably the unusually disturbed state of the country, added to the fear of effreets, was a protection to us, for we anxiously passed several noisy watch-dogs without molestation....

The uplands were gradually declining before us, and to the left we saw only ridges bordering the courses of ravines descending to the bed of the sea. To the right there were other heights with openings through which we could see towards Wady Akabah. In front was the deep ghor, with the bluest of lakes in the hollow, and beyond lay the amethystine mountains of Moab in the afternoon sun. I was too much occupied with the scene to talk. We arrived somewhat abruptly at the precipitous descent, with its ruined fortress below. On the walls of the castle were painted figures like the signs of the Zodiac which seemed of recent date, it was at the foot of this fortress that I was to live with my troop. I dismounted and led the party down the steep descent, while they followed....

I made my plans with Soleiman, and we soon set off, taking the picture case mounted on a donkey to the margin of the sea, that I might choose my place of work and study the sunset effect while drawing in the outline. Glance where we would over the extensive plain and mountains, not a sight of humanity was before us. Getting out of the defile, we turned slightly to the right to reach the spur of Oosdoom, about a mile distant; a furlong beyond that point I made my way to the margin of the sea. There leaving my man to guard the ass, I strode about the hard drifts of the salt-encrusted shallow ridges to find the best site, and wandered to the end of a curve of drift; ten paces away was yet another turn; the salt surface intervening appeared firm enough to trust to with light and rapid steps; I essayed it, but soon found myself sinking into the mire....I threw myself down on the salt surface to secure a wider support, and crawled to the firm ridge. I discovered afterwards there was no danger of sinking much below one's knees. The available spots for painting were now reduced to one or two; when the best had been chosen I employed Soleiman to lead the goat over the surface in order that I might scrutinize its manner of walking on the yielding crust, and the tone of the animal in shadow against the sea and bright distance.

With a few large stones I was able to make a firm foundation for my picture case, and placing another for a seat I proceeded to sketch out the landscape and lines of the composition. Soleiman, when unemployed, upset my gravity by sitting down exactly in front of me in utter bewilderment, staring with open mouth intently into my face.

In an hour I was steadily at work; my man kept repeating the enquiry whether I had finished, but I could not reply. Every minute the mountains became more gorgeous and solemn, the whole scene more unlike any thing ever portrayed. Afar all seemed of the brilliancy and preciousness of jewels, while near, it proved to be only salt and burnt lime, with decayed trees and broken branches brought down by the rivers feeding the lake. Skeletons of animals, which had perished for the most part in crossing the Jordan and the Jabbok, had been swept here and lay salt-covered, so that birds and beasts of prey left them untouched. It was a most appropriate scene for my subject, and each minute I rejoiced more in my work. While thus absorbed, Soleiman touched my arm and said, 'My father, the sunset has come,' and then he grew quite out of patience and added, 'In the dark how can we escape danger? In the light I can detect men from afar, but when the sun has gone, as we go back I can't see if they hide behind trees and shoot us.' I answered, 'My son, be obedient and patient till I have done my work. Keep silent until I am ready, and when I tell you we will hurry back to the tent.'

When the stars were beginning to appear, I removed the ban of silence from the head of my 'son', who was almost in desperation by this time. I tied up the umbrella and shut up my tools, while Soleiman led the donkey. We then together balanced the case on the creature's back, and, securing it, trudged away, not without a trace of ill-humour in my companion. But an Arab soon forgets discontent if you tell him a tale, and by the time we got to the opening in the cliff we were the best of friends....

Each evening I put the sunset glow upon the portion of my day's work, and blocked out the shadows and forms of my painting for the morrow, so that although the effect was, till past mid-day, quite different to what I sought for, I was able, counting with certainty upon a cloudless sunset, to lay in my work, for it was important with the quickly drying paint to complete every atom that I had undertaken, and to make necessary notes for the morrow. My 'son' left the leather water bottle in the shade within reach and wandered about, coming back at lunch-time, when we ate together of bread and fruit and conversed....Lunch finished, I resumed my silent work. I scarcely ever left the spot, even for a few yards knowing how precious time was – more so than I professed to believe – for it was certain that my men, although engaged to stay longer than would be needful, would only by great luck be kept as patient as would be absolutely necessary....

Soon now the mountains, the sea and the middle distance on my canvas were completed, and I was beginning to feel the more indifferent to the grumblings of the men. I was gradually working down to the salt foreground, and one afternoon when Soleiman was away I was pondering on the present state of desolation of 'the way of the sea', when my 'brother' appeared, looking more impressive than usual. He crouched down beside me, put his hand out to the cliffs towards Masada, and uttered the portentous words, 'There are robbers; they are coming this way – one, two, three, on horseback, and two – wait, three – yes, four on foot. They have not yet seen us, and soon they will be behind Oosdoom, and we shall be able safely to move. You must put down your umbrella, shut up your picture, cover it with stones. They will not be here for an hour. We will go up in the mountain; they will keep along the road at the foot; we will come back to the picture when they have gone by.' I could see the party very far away and asked, 'How do you know they are robbers?' 'They are always robbers when the others are feeble; it would be useless for us to resist. Quick,' he said. 'Perhaps they belong to a friendly tribe,' I argued. 'They do not,' he said. 'Come.' 'No,' I said, 'I shall stay.' He implored me to listen and finally stamped, saying, 'Your blood be on your own head; as for me I shall go to the mountain and hide myself.' As he went away he turned two or three times, and again appealed to me like a man at his wits' end. 'Why stay? What do you trust in?' I replied mine was a good work, that Allah would

'The Scapegoat'

help me, and that I was content to accept whatever might be the issue, and I saw him run to the break in the mountain near, and, with the ass, climb up its roughness and disappear.

I worked on steadily, but had to turn my head occasionally to watch the progress of the deeshman....I suspended my painting and looked from beneath my umbrella, until suddenly the deeshman emerged from behind the mountain within half a furlong of me where they all halted. The horsemen had their faces covered with black kufeyiahs, and carried long spears, while the footmen carried guns, swords and clubs. They stood stock-still some minutes, pointing at my umbrella, and then turned out of the beaten way direct to me, clattering at a measured pace among the large and loose stones. I continued placidly conveying my paint from palette to canvas, steadying my touch by resting the hand on my double-barrelled gun. I knew that my whole chance depended upon the exhibition of utter unconcern, and I continued as steadily as if in my studio at home.

Eventually the whole party drew up in a half-circle. The leader thundered out, 'Give me some water.' I turned and looked at him from his head to his horse's feet, and then very deliberately at the others, and resumed my task without saying a word. He stormed again, 'Do you hear? Give us some water.' After turning to him once more with a little pause, extending my right hand on my breast, I said, 'I am an Englishman; you are an Arab. Englishmen are not the servants of Arabs; I am employing Arabs for servants. You are thirsty – it is hot – the water is there – I will out of kindness let you have some, but you must help one another; I have something else to do,' and I turned again quietly to work....

The demands for interviews with me at night on my return from work were frequent, both from Bedouin and muleteers; their object always was to shorten our stay. Our food supply could not be replenished, for no one would go back to the Jehalin encampment to buy provisions. I pointed out they ought to have provided food not only for a fortnight but for two months, and it was their lack of prudence only that was to blame. Still, that the animals had insufficient food was not triumphantly parried by the fact that I also participated in the famine, my mukary now persisted that he would take all his troop back in a few days without me, if I would not come. My counter proposal was that he should go the next day with the luggage, the canteen included, and even my riding horse and Nicola's [a muleteer], that we should have only one mule to carry the picture and a few blankets and cooking things, and that Nicola and I should walk the whole way to Jerusalem, but the fellow would not even consent to this.

Under the most favourable circumstances Nature exhibits her jealousy in frustrating all attempts of the artist to represent her, but in Syria it seemed that she obtained allies of such strength to fight her battles that it needed superhuman patience to continue the struggle against her; I held in reserve the fact that I had nearly finished my background except such parts as clouds and other details sketched, which could be as well completed in Jerusalem....

In shifting the picture in and out of the case, it was strange in this wild place to read on the back the name of the colourman with the address, 51 Long Acre; now there was nothing essential for me to paint but the driftwood and adjacent salt, and this I brought happily to an end. After sunset I announced to Soleiman that I had finished. Collecting salt and one or two other relics for use in Jerusalem, we returned to the tent prepared to start on the morrow....

Soon after sunrise my own preparations were complete. Sad at leaving the place I consoled myself with the promise that I would soon return from England and paint the castle and some other wonderful scenes about the wady....I led my horse up the difficult slope, full of thanksgiving at having so far been able to achieve my object in the expedition. It was a blessing to get on the broad upland again, release from prison, and the sweet breezes welcomed me from the tropical-heated plain.

# CHARLES LEONARD IRBY

## 1789–1845

*Tiberias (steel engraving by Harry Fenn, 1873)*

*Charles Leonard Irby was born in 1789. He entered the navy in 1801, was promoted to lieutenant in 1808 and then served on the coast of North America. In 1814 he was promoted to the command of the Thames and took part in the unfortunate expedition against New Orleans. Ill-health forced him to resign his command in May 1815. In the summer of 1816 he left England with his friend, James Mangles, and journeyed across the continent, then on to Egypt, up the Nile, across the desert and, with a detour to Baalbeck and Aleppo, finally to Jerusalem. Whilst there, they participated in what was probably the first recorded attempt to excavate the ruins of Jerusalem, described below. Despite every obstacle put in their way, they then managed to make the perilous journey round the Dead Sea to Petra. The letters written during their journey were privately printed in 1823 and then published in 1844 under the title* Travels in Egypt and Nubia, Syria and the Holy Land. *From 1826 to 1828 Irby was back in command of a ship, but after that he had no further service. He died in February 1845.*

*Tiberias*
*26 February 1818*

We were detained [at Safed] by rainy weather, until the afternoon of the 28th, when we started for Tiberias, but only reached an old ruined khan, about two miles to the north of the village of Madjala by the lake's side. Here we were dreadfully bitten by a species of vermin, which attacks both men and camels in this country; it was red and soft like a maggot. In the morning we found ourselves studded all over with deep crimson spots, from which it would appear that there is much venom in the bite of this disgusting animal. A traveller in these countries, however much the thought may shock him at first, must make up his mind to be constantly covered with lice and fleas; we kill every day from ten to twenty of these gentry, which are always to be found on every mat or cushion used in the country. These nauseous visitors seldom get into the head, but crawl about your shirt and clothes. Every native you see is covered with them, and if you ask why they have such a plentiful store, while we are comparatively so little attacked, they tell you 'it is the curse of God on them'....

*1 March:* The greater part of our road this day was a descent, passing through a beautiful and wild country covered with shrubs of various descriptions, and occasionally crossing valleys and rivulets. About four miles from Safed there is a picturesque cliff, the sides of which are perforated with a great number of caves, at present inhabited by goatherds; we supposed them to be ancient sepulchres, as indeed did other travellers who, from their ruined appearance, have not thought them worthy of examination; but Mr Bankes, who leaves nothing unexplored, inspected them and pronounces them to be only natural cavities. About eight o'clock we reached Tiberias, having travelled for two hours along the side of the lake. More pains have appeared to be taken to construct a road where it was very rocky than in most parts of Syria which we visited. The modern town of Tiberias is very small; it stands close to the lake of Gennesareth and is walled round with towers equidistant to each other. At the northern extremity are the remains of the ancient town, which are distinguishable by walls and other ruined buildings, as well as by fragments of columns, some of which are of beautiful red granite. South of the town are the famous hot baths of Tiberias; they consist of three mineral springs. We had no thermometer, but we found the water too hot to admit of the hand being kept in it for more than fifty seconds; we endeavoured to boil an egg in it, but without success, even though we removed the shell. Over the spring is a Turkish bath close to the lake's side, which is much resorted to, particularly by the Jews, who have also a great veneration for a Roman sepulchre, excavated in the cliff near the spot, which they say is the 'Tomb of Jacob'. Beyond the baths a wall runs from the lake to the mountain's side, which rather perplexed us when we were taking the measurement of the ancient walls of Tiberias; but we are now convinced that this wall did not extend so far to the south, and that this wall was part of the fortifications of Vespasian's camp; indeed Josephus places the camp in this position. The lake of Tiberias is a fine sheet of water, but the land about it has no striking features and the scenery is altogether devoid of beauty; but it is interesting from the frequent allusions to it in the Gospels. We were lodged, as Frank travellers usually are, in the small catholic church, which is under the charge of an Arab priest; this they tell you was the house of St Peter; but after we had been there a few days, we observed that one of the stones of the building had part of an Arabic inscription upon it, inverted, which proves it to be of much more modern origin.... We found the church so full of fleas that we preferred a small open court in front of it for our lodging. The natives have a saying, that 'the king of the fleas has his court in Tabaria'. We here lived on fish, which is most excellent; there is not much variety, but the best sort, and it is the most common, is a species of bream, equal to the finest perch. It is remarkable that there is not, at present, a single boat of any description on the lake; the fish are caught by the casting-net from the beach, a method which must yield a very small quantity compared to what would be obtained from boats. I imagine that this is the reason why fish is so dear....

### Adventure at the 'Tombs of the Kings', Jerusalem
### 2 May 1818

A rather singular adventure befell us while at Jerusalem. There is amongst the sepulchres, which travellers have designated as 'The Tombs of the Kings', an excavated vault with an oblong portico. The only visible entrance to this vault is at one end of the portico, while from its construction there is every reason to suppose that a corresponding entrance would be found at the other end, which is now filled with rubbish. Mr Bankes was so thoroughly convinced of this, that when at Constantinople he used every exertion, but in vain, to procure a firman authorizing him to excavate and ascertain the fact. We now endeavoured to obtain permission from the Governor of Jerusalem to dig there, but without success. As we could not procure legal authority, we determined on prosecuting the undertaking secretly in the night, and accordingly purchased privately some pickaxes and other implements. Late in the evening we quitted the town, singly and from different gates, to avoid suspicion; and assembling at the rendezvous after dark, found that we mustered a party of ten persons ... together with five servants, including two of Lord Belmore's sailors, whom his Lordship had allowed to join us. We divided our party into two watches, and worked hard four hours at a time during the whole night, digging and clearing away the rubbish. We were obliged to station one of the servants as a sentinel near the road side, to apprise us of the approach of anyone. In the morning we had removed the rubbish to a depth of about ten feet, when we came to an immense block of stone, apparently in the very spot where we expected to find the entrance to the tomb. As we were unable to move this mass, we returned to the city, pretty well fatigued, having been obliged, for want of spades, to clear away the rubbish with our hands. The next day Captain Corry, Mr Bankes and Mahomet his janissary, acting on the suggestion of Lord Belmore, succeeded in breaking the stone by heating it, and then pouring cold vinegar on it but, unfortunately, shortly after this was done, our proceedings were discovered by some Turks and reported to the Governor, who put a very effectual stop to our researches, by ordering the whole of the portico to be walled in.

### Preparations for the Journey to Petra
### May 1818

Great were the obstacles which presented themselves, and innumerable the difficulties which we had to surmount before we could commence our journey to Petra....

...When Mr Bankes applied at Constantinople to have Kerak and Wady Mousa inserted in his firman, the Turkish government returned for answer, 'that they knew of no such place within the Grand Seigneur's dominions'; but as he and Mr Frere, the British minister, pressed the point very much, they at length referred him to the Pasha of Damascus, who, equally averse to have anything to do with the business, passed him on to the Governor of Jerusalem. This latter tried all he could to dissuade us from the undertaking, though Mr

Legh gave him a handsome spy-glass to induce him to assist us. He advised us to apply to Mahommed Aga, the Governor of Jaffa. The communication between Egypt and Mousa being usually through Gaza, which is under Mohammed Aga's government, it was supposed that he would have the greatest influence over the Arabs of Wady Mousa, inasmuch as he possessed the means of punishing them for any violence they might commit, either by stopping their supplies from Egypt, or making them prisoners of such of their people as came within his reach. The Governor of Jaffa, however, not only evaded the affair altogether, but, in order to put a stop to our journey, ordered us to return the horses which he had lent us. A second visit to the Governor of Jerusalem seemed to promise as little as the preceding. We all four called on him. On this occasion, a former mussulman, who had been twenty years in office, and was sitting with the Governor, pledged his word to us that the Arabs are a most savage and treacherous race; and to prove it, added, that they think Franks' blood a good medicine for their women when sick, and that they would make use of ours for this purpose. All that we could procure from the governor was a promise to write to the Sheikh of Kerak to apprise him of our coming....Finding that there was no getting any of the public authorities to render us any assistance, we determined to proceed, trusting to our numbers and force, and to try our fortune with the Sheikh of Hebron. Each of the party procured a Bedouin Arab dress of the most ordinary description and we all bought horses for the journey....We took the precaution of having as little baggage as possible with us, and sent the greater part to Acre with one of Mr Legh's servants. We assumed Eastern names for the journey: Mr Legh was called Osman; Mr Bankes, Halleel; Captain Irby, Abdallah....Our dress consisted of a frock and drawers of very coarse linen; the frock being fastened round the waist by a red leathern girdle, about four inches broad. The head-dress was a handkerchief of mixed silk and cotton, coloured with broad stripes of alternate red, green and yellow. This was doubled into a triangular form and thrown over the head, to which it was attached by a double girdle of brown worsted rope. One corner of the handkerchief hangs down over the back of the neck, the other two cover the ears and come down over the shoulders. When the weather is cold, the Arabs tuck up these corners under the chin and cover the whole face with the exception of the eyes. Over all we had the woollen abba, which we had long worn, and which we had procured at Jaffa. As regards arms, we had amongst us six muskets, one blunderbus, five braces of pistols and two sabres. Our money, consisting of small gold coins, was concealed in leather belts round our waists next to the skin.

In the evening of the 6th of May we left Jerusalem....

# ALEXANDER KINGLAKE

## ⬧ 1809–91 ⬧

*Alexander Kinglake, c.1863 (portrait by H.M. Haviland)*

Born in Somerset on 5 August 1809, Alexander Kinglake was educated at Eton and Trinity College, Cambridge. He was called to the Bar in 1837, but cared little for his profession. In 1835 he made the Eastern tour which he so vividly described afterwards in his book, Eothen, or Traces of Travel, which was finally published in 1844 after having been rewritten by the author three times. This quickly became established as one of the most popular books on Eastern travel and was hailed as a classic of its genre. Having always been interested in military history, Kinglake went to Algiers in 1845 and accompanied the flying column of St Arnaud; and in 1854 he followed the English expedition to the Crimea and was present at the battle of the Alma. In 1856 he began writing the history of the campaign and the first two volumes of his History of the War in the Crimea were published in 1863. The remaining six volumes later appeared between 1868 and 1887, and soon became recognized as one of the finest historical works of the century. In 1857 he was elected as a Liberal to Parliament and held the seat for Bridgwater until 1868, after which he was fully occupied with his historical writing right up until his death in 1891.

*Terra Santa*

The enthusiasm that had glowed, or seemed to glow, within me, for one blessed moment, when I knelt by the shrine of the Virgin at Nazareth, was not rekindled at Jerusalem. In the stead of the solemn gloom, and the deep stillness that of right belonged to the Holy City, there was the hum and the bustle of active life. It was the 'height of the season'. The Easter ceremonies drew near; the pilgrims were flocking in from all quarters, and although their objects were partly at least of a religious character, yet their 'arrivals' brought as much stir and liveliness to the city, as if they had come up to marry their daughters.

The votaries who every year crowd to the Holy Sepulchre are chiefly of the Greek and Armenian churches. They are not drawn into Palestine by a mere sentimental longing to stand upon the ground trodden by our Saviour, but rather they perform the pilgrimage as a plain duty strongly inculcated by their religion. A very great proportion of those who belong to the Greek Church, contrive at some time or other, in the course of their lives, to achieve the enterprise. Many in their infancy and childhood are brought to the holy sites by their parents, but those who have not had this advantage will often make it the main object of their lives to save money enough for this holy undertaking.

The pilgrims begin to arrive in Palestine some weeks before the Easter festival of the Greek Church; they come from Egypt – from all parts of Syria – from Armenia, and Asia Minor – from Istambul, from Roumelia, from the provinces of the Danube, and from all the Russias. Most of these people bring with them some articles of merchandise, but I myself believe (notwithstanding the common taunt against pilgrims) that they do this rather as a mode of paying the expenses of their journey, than from a spirit of mercenary speculation; they generally travel in families, for the women are of course more ardent than their husbands in undertaking these pious enterprises, and they take care to bring with them all their children, however young, for the efficacy of the rites does not depend upon the age of the votary, so that people whose careful mothers have obtained for them the benefit of the pilgrimage in early life, are saved from the expense and trouble of undertaking the journey at a later age. The superior veneration so often excited by objects that are distant and unknown sheds not perhaps the wrongheadedness of a man, but rather the transcendent power of his Imagination....

The great bulk of the pilgrims make their way by sea to the port of Jaffa. A number of families will charter a vessel amongst them, all bringing their own provisions, which are of the simplest and cheapest kind. On board every vessel thus freighted, there is, I believe, a priest, who helps the people in their religious exercises, and tries (and fails) to maintain something like order and harmony. The vessels employed in this service are usually Greek brigs, or brigantines, and schooners, and the number of passengers stowed in them is almost always horribly excessive. The voyages are sadly protracted, not only by the land-seeking, storm-flying habits of the Greek seamen, but also by their endless schemes and speculations, which are for ever tempting them to touch at the nearest port. The voyage, too, must be made in winter, in order that Jerusalem may be reached some weeks before the Greek Easter, and thus by the time they attain to the holy shrines, the pilgrims have really and truly undergone a very respectable quantity of suffering....

When the pilgrims have landed at Jaffa, they hire camels, horses, mules or donkeys, and make their way as well as they can to the Holy City. The space fronting the Church of the Holy Sepulchre, soon becomes a kind of bazaar, or rather perhaps reminds you of an English fair. On this spot the pilgrims display their merchandise, and there too the trading residents of the place offer their goods for sale. I have never, I think, seen elsewhere in Asia so much commercial animation as upon this square of ground by the church door; the 'money changers' seemed to be almost as brisk and lively as if they had been within the Temple.

When I entered the Church, I found a Babel of worshippers. Greek, Roman and Armenian priests were performing their different rites in various nooks and corners, and crowds of disciples were rushing about in all directions – some laughing and talking, some begging, but most of them going round in a regular and methodical way to kiss the sanctified spots, and speak the appointed syllables, and lay down the accustomed coin. If this kissing of the shrines had seemed as though it were done at the bidding of Enthusiasm, or of any poor sentiment even feebly approaching to it, the sight would have been less odd to English eyes; but as it was, I stared to see grown men thus steadily and carefully embracing the sticks and the stones – not from love or from zeal (else God forbid that I should have stared), but from a calm sense of duty; they seemed to be not 'working out', but transacting the great business of Salvation....

A Protestant, familiar with the Holy Scriptures, but ignorant of tradition and the geography of modern Jerusalem, finds himself a good deal 'mazed' when he first looks for the sacred sites. The Holy Sepulchre is not in a field without the walls, but in the midst, and in the best part of the town, under the roof of the great Church which I have been talking about; it is a handsome tomb of oblong form, partly subterranean and partly above ground; and closed in on all sides, except the one by which it is entered. You descend into the interior by a few steps, and there find an altar with burning tapers. This is the spot which is held in greater sanctity than any other at Jerusalem. When you have seen enough of it, you feel perhaps weary of the busy crowd and inclined for a gallop; you ask your dragoman whether there will be time before sunset to procure horses and take a ride to Mount Calvary. Mount Calvary, Signor? – eccolo! it is upstairs – on the first floor. In effect you ascend, if I remember rightly, just thirteen steps, and then you are shown the now golden sockets in which the crosses of our Lord and the two thieves were fixed. All this is startling, but the truth is that the city having gathered round the Sepulchre, which is the main point of interest, has crept northward, and thus in great measure are occasioned the many geographical surprises that puzzle the 'Bible Christian'.

The Church of the Holy Sepulchre comprises very compendiously almost all the spots associated with the closing career of our Lord. Just there, on your right, he stood and wept; by the pillar on your left he was scourged; on the spot just before you he was crowned with the crown of thorns; up there he was crucified, and down here he was buried. A locality is assigned to every the minutest event connected with the recorded history of our Saviour; even the spot where the cock crew when Peter denied his Master is ascertained and surrounded by the walls of an Armenian convent. Many Protestants are wont to treat these traditions contemptuously, and those who distinguish themselves from their brethren by the appellation of 'Bible Christians' are almost fierce in their denunciation of these supposed errors.

It is admitted, I believe, by everybody, that the formal sanctification of these spots was the act of the Empress Helena, the mother of Constantine, but I think it is fair to suppose that she was guided by a careful regard to the then prevailing traditions. Now the nature of the ground upon which Jerusalem stands is such that the localities belonging to the events there enacted might have been more easily and permanently ascertained by tradition, than those of any city that I know of. Jerusalem, whether ancient or modern, was built upon and surrounded by sharp, salient rocks, intersected by deep ravines. Up to the time of the siege, Mount Calvary of course must have been well-enough known to the people of Jerusalem; the destruction of the mere buildings could not have obliterated from any man's memory the names of those steep rocks and narrow ravines in the midst of which the city had stood.

It seems to me therefore highly probable that in fixing the site of Calvary, the Empress was rightly guided. Recollect, too, that the voice of tradition at Jerusalem is quite unanimous, and that Romans, Greeks, Armenians and Jews, all hating each other sincerely, concur in assigning the same localities to the events told in the Gospel. I concede, however, that the attempt of the Empress to ascertain the sites of the minor events cannot be safely relied upon. With respect, for instance, to the certainty of the spot where the cock crew, I am far from being convinced....

## The Girls of Bethlehem

You know what a sad and sombre decorum it is that outwardly reigns through the lands oppressed by Moslem sway. The Mohammedans make beauty their prisoner and enforce such a stern and gloomy morality, or at all events such a frightfully close semblance of it, that far and long the wearied traveller may go, without catching one glimpse of outward happiness. By a strange chance in these latter days, it happened that alone of all the places in this land, this Bethlehem, the native village of our Lord, escaped the moral yoke of the Mussulmans and heard again, after ages of oppression, the cheering clatter of social freedom and the voices of laughing girls....

...when you see and hear them, those romping girls of Bethlehem will gladden your very soul. Distant at first, and then nearer and nearer the timid flock will gather around you with their large burning eyes gravely fixed against yours, so that they see into your brain, and if you imagine evil against them they will know of your ill thought before it is yet well born, and will fly and be gone in the moment. But presently, if you will only look virtuous enough to prevent alarm, and vicious enough to avoid looking silly, the blithe maidens will draw nearer and nearer to you, and soon there will be one, the bravest of the sisters, who will venture right up to your side and touch the hem of your coat in playful defiance of the danger, and then the rest will follow the daring of their youthful leader and gather close round you, and hold a shrill controversy on the wondrous formation that you call a hat, and the cunning of the hands that clothed you with cloth so fine; and then growing more profound in their researches, they will pass from the study of your mere dress to a serious contemplation of your stately height and your nut-brown hair, and the ruddy glow of your English cheeks. And if they catch a glimpse of your ungloved fingers, then again will they make the air ring with their sweet screams of wonder and amazement, as they compare the fairness of your hand with their warmer tints, and even with the hues of your own sunburnt face; instantly the ringleader of the gentle rioters imagines a new sin; with tremulous boldness she touches – then grasps your hand, and smooths it gently betwixt her own, and prys curiously into its make and colour, as though it were silk of Damascus, or a shawl of Cashmere....

'I regret to observe that the removal of the moral restraint imposed by the presence of the Mohammedan inhabitants has led to a certain degree of boisterous, though innocent levity, in the bearing of the Christians, and more especially in the demeanour of those who belong to the younger portion of the female population, but I feel assured that a more thorough knowledge of the principles of their own pure religion, will speedily restore these young people to habits of propriety, even more strict than those which were imposed upon them by the authority of their Mohammedan brethren.' Bah! thus you might chant, if you chose; but loving the truth, you will not so disown sweet Bethlehem – you will not disown or dissemble your right good hearty delight, when you find, as though in a desert, this gushing spring of fresh and joyous girlhood.

*The Girls of Bethlehem*

# HORATIO HERBERT KITCHENER

## 1850–1916

*Horatio Herbert Kitchener, 1890 (portrait by H. von Herkome)*

Horatio Herbert Kitchener was born in 1850 near Ballylongford, Kerry. He joined the Royal Military Academy in 1868 and entered the Royal Engineers in 1871. In 1874 he was lent to the Palestine Exploration Fund to help with the survey of western Palestine – a connection with the East which was to last all of his life. The expedition had to be halted in July 1875 after a murderous attack on the surveying party by the Moslem inhabitants of Safed, in which he bravely defended his superior, Lieutenant Condor (described below). The survey was finally completed in 1877. In 1878, when Great Britain acquired Cyprus, he was sent to survey the island and, in 1883, he devoted two months' leave to survey the Sinai Peninsula. The following year, during the insurrection of the Sudanese under the Mahdi, he was sent up the Nile to try to establish communication with Berber, which was besieged by the Mahdists, and then with General Gordon in Khartoum – but, by then, it was too late to relieve him. Appointed Sirdar of the Egyptian army in 1890, he had won the Sudan back for Egypt by the final rout of the Khalifar at Omdurman in

September 1898. As a result he was made a peer. From 1902–9 he was Chief of Staff and Commander-in-Chief in South Africa, and at the end of the Boer War he was made a viscount, received the Order of Merit and appointed Consul-General in Egypt (1911). In August 1914 he was made Secretary of State for War, but, although he organized a great army, British munitions supplies were both insufficient and inefficient. As a result, he was replaced at the War Office in 1915. A year later he was drowned when the ship he was travelling in, HMS Hampshire, was sunk.

*The Safed Attack*
*A Letter from Lt Conder to the Consul-General of Beirut, 14 July 1875*

Sir ... On Saturday, the 10th July, we arrived about 4 p.m. at Safed, from 'El Ba'ineh', and erected our tents on a piece of uncultivated ground under olives near 'Ain el Beida, north of the Moslem quarter. A number of Moslems became spectators of our proceedings. A small English tent was being erected when many of these persons, including one who dressed in a turban and white abba, came down to it and began in a very insolent manner to examine it, laying their fingers on everything and behaving with marked want of courtesy and respect. I am informed that they said they had seen 'many dogs like us before'.

A ten-chambered revolver, hanging on a tree by the tent, was missed at this moment, and its owner, one of my servants, began to enquire whether anyone had seen it. I am informed that the leader of the Moslems cursed him in reply. At this moment I came out of my tent where I was resting, and heard my head servant address this man with civility, using the expression hadrabuk, and telling him to go away, as it was not his business. I heard the sheikh reply violently with imprecations, and saw him fling two or perhaps three very large stones at my head servant. The latter did not reply by violence, but took the bystanders to witness that an unprovoked assault had been made upon him. I advanced as quickly as I could without arms and with nothing in my hands. Before I spoke a single word the sheikh seized me violently by the throat. In defence I struck him in the face with my fist and knocked him down. He got up and again assaulted me, when I struck him right and left, and cut open his lip. When on the ground he drew a knife, which measures half a foot length of blade. My head servant fortunately saw him just before he stabbed me, and two of my people took it away from him and seized him, intending to retain him until the arrival of the government officials. They also bound him, but not by my order....

I ordered the sheikh to be immediately released, but he refused at first to leave the camp, though he subsequently retired for arms. Meanwhile he encouraged his people to kill all the Christians.

They began by a shower of enormous stones upon our party, which only numbered fifteen persons, of whom two were ill at the time.

Lieutenant Kitchener and myself, supported by our three non-commissioned officers, none having any firearms or other offensive weapon in our hands or about our persons, endeavoured to calm the disturbance and to separate the crowd from our servants, who, infuriated at the treatment I had received, were anxious, in spite of their small numbers, to attack the Moslems. The five Europeans were in imminent danger of their lives from the falling stones. Whilst thus engaged, Lieutenant Kitchener was seriously injured on the thigh with a huge stone....

At this moment there arrived a number of armed men, apparently the sheikhs of the quarter, who encouraged the crowd. Of those, one man had a large scimitar and a carbine, another a battle-axe; two had large clubs (dabbus), and another a long gun. To these weapons I can swear and believe there were many more.

Lieutenant Kitchener and I were immediately surrounded. Three came to me and asked with curses what I was doing. An old man thrust his battle-axe violently into my side, but I did not like to strike him, though I had now a hunting crop in my hand. I told them they were mad and would be severely punished if they struck an Englishman. About this time other members of the party saw a gun levelled at me five yards off, but fortunately the man's hand was caught before he fired. A man now came into the crowd which surrounded me, and dealt me a blow on the head with a large club with great violence, causing two wounds on the side of my head, covering my face with blood. A second blow, directed with full force at the top of my head, must inevitably have brained me had I not put my head down to his chest. My servants gave me up for dead....As soon as I got up I dealt this man a blow in the face with the handle of my whip which staggered him, but my whip flew out of my hand and left me entirely unarmed. I must inevitably have been murdered but for the cool and prompt assistance of Lieutenant Kitchener, who managed to get to me and engaged one of the club men, covering my retreat.

A blow descending on the top of his head he parried with a cane, which was broken by the force of the blow. A second wounded his arm. His escape is unaccountable. Having retired a few paces from the thick of the fray, I saw that the Moslems were gradually surrounding us, stealing behind trees and through vineyards, and I well understood that in such a case, unless the soldiers arrived at once, we must all die. Many of the servants had indeed already given up hope, though no one fled. I gave the order to leave the tents and fly round the hill.

Lieutenant Kitchener was the last to obey this order, being engaged in front. He retreated to his tent, and whilst running he was fired at, and heard the bullet whistle by his head. He was also followed for some short distance by a man with a huge scimitar, who subsequently wounded with it more than one of our people.

Gaining the cover of some trees, we stopped on a bare hill-side to consult, and ventured back to the brow to reconnoitre. At this moment the soldiers arrived with an officer and the English consular-agent, Marcus Cigal. I am informed that all the offensive weapons were immediately concealed, the stoning and blasphemous language ceased at once, and not an individual of the crowd remained....

*Palestine Survey Camp, Haifa*
*6 March 1877*

... Owing to the lateness of the rainy season this year the country is still in a very swampy condition and, even had we not been unavoidably delayed, work could hardly have been begun before. The Kishon has to be crossed in a boat, the horses and mules swimming, and as we have had to cross it twice every day it has caused great loss of time. The first day we found considerable difficulty in crossing the Plain of Acca owing to the marshy nature of the ground after the late rains, and could only get to our work by making a long detour after some of us had experienced the pleasures of a mud bath. We were also delayed one day by wet weather.

I have also made a strict enquiry after the name of 'Kulmon' or 'Kalamon'....The German colony here have purchased nearly all the land north of Tireh, and I have been allowed to carefully examine their title-deeds; though they have land all round Khurbet Kefr es Samir, no such name occurs.

I have also ridden to Tireh with the sole object of finding this name. I asked everyone I met on the road there and back, about twenty people, first for all the names of the country round, and, as a last resource, if they had every heard of 'Kulmon', 'Kulamon' or anything like it. At Kh. Kefr es Samir I found an old man who inhabited a cave close by and put the

*Capernaum – one of the sites surveyed by Kitchener in 1877*

same question. At Tireh I saw the sheikh and about two dozen men; none had ever heard of such a name. Since then the superior of the convent of Mount Carmel, who knows the district most thoroughly, has assured me that no such name occurs. I can therefore only assume that the name does not exist, and that our map is therefore right in not putting it on. How other maps procured the name seems difficult to understand; but, as in some other case, it may have been supplied by some too enthusiastic traveller, who looked more for what ought to be in the country than what is.

*Camp at Jerusalem*
*2 October 1877*

On the 12th September we left Jerusalem with the object of surveying the desert between Gaza and Beersheba. Our first day's march was to Hebron, where I attached two soldiers to the expedition....I found out here that the next village I was going to, Dhoheriyeh, was entirely deserted. Owing to the bad year, the inhabitants were not able to pay taxes and found it better to desert their homes. There is also a great want of water in the country.

I therefore changed my plans and marched to Beit Jibrin. Here we found barley and provisions very dear, owing to the bad harvest. I could learn little or nothing about the country I was going to, as the fellahin and Arabs have always a feud with each other, and neither dare venture into the other's territory. However, I found out that there was water at Tell el Hesy and encamped there. We were now entirely in the Arab country, having left all villages some hours behind us. The principal sheikh of the Jubarât Arabs, Sheikh 'Aid ed Dibs, was made to a certain extent responsible for anything that might be stolen.

The whole country was as bare as a freshly ploughed field, and far from being a dead level, as shown on existing maps, not a tree or house to be seen in the wide prospect of rolling ground. In the spring, however, all this country is green with barley. Last year the crops entirely failed. We had luckily come to the only place with water for many miles round, and here it was very brackish and the colour of weak tea.

On Saturday, the 15th, we started the triangulation and were able to finish in one day after observing from three points. On Monday the surveying commenced. Our Arab guides were a cause of some difficulty, as they were afraid of our going far south and were most exorbitant in their demands for bakshish. Luckily it is Ramadan, the month in which the Moslems are not allowed to eat or drink while the sun is up, so that we escaped being obliged to feed a large number of visitors.

All the week the work went on steadily. Coming back from the south, or enemy's country, in the evening, we often scared the Arabs with their flocks of camels, and once Corporal Brophy was charged by an Arab with a spear to within inches of his face.

Our principal discovery was the ruins of Ziklag, which still bears the name of Khurbet Zuheilîkah. Lieutenant Conder first heard the name and suggested the identification. The ruins occur on three small hills in the form of an equilateral triangle, nearly half a mile apart. The highest hill of the three is to the north and forms the apex of the triangle. There are a number of ancient ruined cisterns at the ruins, but as in almost every case in this part of the country, the stones have all been removed, the sites ploughed over, and they are only visible now by the white patches on the dark soil, which show well even at a distance at this time of year, though in the spring they are completely hid by the crops. The site is in the open rolling plain, some distance from the low hills of the Shefalah. It is eleven miles distant from Gaza....

On the 26th we moved camp to Bir es Seba. We had been warned of some danger from the Arabs in this part, but found the country entirely feared by both tribes, therefore neither dare venture into it except for raids. We had considerable difficulty about the names, and I am convinced that in less troubled times more might be collected in this part....

Our journey back was rapid, owing to all our bread having gone mouldy and our provisions run short. Our first day took us to Dura on the road. At the wells near El Burg some fellahin were watering their flocks of goats. Seeing a mounted party arriving from the Bedouin country, they raised a shout of 'Bedouins!' Away went the goats at a gallop up the hills. This we were used to and rode on trying to reassure them by shouting 'Soldiers!' when about fifteen men ran together behind some stone walls and, after gesticulating frantically, opened fire upon us. The balls whistled by and threw up the dust under our horses' feet, so we pulled up, and after some difficulty succeeded in making them understand who we were. After all, we ran more danger from our friends than from the much-dreaded Arabs. At Dura some boys threw stones at Corporal Sutherland, so I had them publicly flogged.

Next day, Saturday, we marched into Jerusalem, our horses rather done up by their hard work. Our tents and camels did not arrive till after dark. We shall now have about a fortnight's work preparing everything in duplicate. I will then send home the last portion of the map and take up the work of revision....

# Alphonse Marie Louis de Lamartine

**1790–1868**

*Alphonse de Lamartine*

*Alphonse de Lamartine was born on 21 October 1790 at Mâcon. His family were minor aristocracy and he was brought up with ultra-royalist principles. He spent much of his youth in Italy and on the fall of Napoleon joined the garde royale. In 1816, at Aix-les-Bains, he fell in love with Mme Julie Charles, who died the following year. She became the chief inspiration for his poems and his first volume, Méditations poétiques, published in 1820, became his most successful and best-known work, and established him as one of the leading figures in the French Romantic movement. From the late 1820s his work was widely translated into English. He moved to Naples as secretary of the legation and became chargé d'affaires at Florence in 1825, where he served for three years. In 1829 he declined the post of foreign secretary in the Polignac ministry, and by another series of poems, Harmonies poétiques et religieuses, achieved his unanimous election to the French Academy. Still a royalist, he disapproved of the revolution in 1830 and in 1832 set off on a year's tour of the East, the account of which was published in his Souvenirs d'Orient. Recalled to France, he became deputy for Mâcon. Between 1834 and 1848 he published his poems, Jocelyn and La Chute d'un Age, and the celebrated Histoire des Girondins. This eight-volume history helped to incite the revolution of 1848, after which he became a member of the provisional government and, as Minister of Foreign Affairs, its ruling spirit. After a terrible conflict, the insurrection was suppressed and, when Louis Napoleon came to power, Lamartine decided to devote himself to literature. The remaining years of his life – he died in Paris in February 1869 – were spent in writing autobiographical works (Confidences and Raphael), a history of the revolution, a novel, Graziella, a prose tale and several other historical books. In debt during the later part of his life, he compiled a twenty-eight volume Cours familier de littérature 1856–69), in an attempt to pay off his creditors.*

Abou Gosh
October 1832

We set out again before daybreak, following, during two hours, a narrow valley, barren and rocky, celebrated for the depredations of the Arabs. Of all the neighbourhood, this spot is the most exposed to their incursions; they may approach it by numerous little winding valleys concealed behind uninhabited hills; and lie there in ambush, hidden by the rocks and shrubs, ready to pounce upon a caravan at the first unguarded moment. The celebrated Abou Gosh, chief of the Arab tribes of these mountains, holds the key of these defiles which lead to Jerusalem; he opens or closes them at his pleasure, and ransoms travellers. His headquarters were at some leagues from us at the village of Jeremy....

We met on an uncultivated open space in front of the village, shaded by five or six fine fig trees....

He advanced towards me with his brother only: his suite remaining behind. I immediately halted mine and approached him, with my interpreter. After the usual salutations, and the interminable compliments which precede all conversation with the Arabs, Abou Gosh asked me if I was not the French emir whom his friend, Lady H. Stanhope, the Queen of Palmyra, had recommended to his protection and in whose name she had sent him the superb vest of gold tissue, which he then wore and which he showed me with pride and gratitude. I was ignorant of this gift which Lady Hester had so obligingly made him in my name; but I answered that I was indeed the foreigner whom this illustrious lady had recommended to the generosity of her friends at Jeremy; that I was going to traverse all Palestine, where the dominion of Abou Gosh was recognized, and that I entreated him to give such orders, that Lady Hester might have nothing to reproach him with.

At these words he alighted from his horse, as did his brother; he called to him some of his suite, ordered them to bring mats, carpets and cushions, which he made them spread under the shadow of a great fig tree, on the spot where we were standing, and so warmly pressed us to alight and take our seats upon this rustic divan, that it was impossible to refuse. As the plague was in Jeremy, Abou Gosh, who knew that all Europeans were in quarantine, took care not to touch our clothes, and established his divan, and that of his brother, opposite to us, at a certain distance: for ourselves, we accepted only mats of straw and rush, because they are reputed not to communicate infection. Coffee and sherbet were brought....'Is my name known in Europe?' he asked. 'Yes,' I answered; 'by some you are represented as a robber, pillaging and massacring caravans, leading the Franks into slavery, and the ferocious enemy of the Christians; while others assert that you are a valiant and generous prince, respecting the depredations of the Arabs of the mountains, giving security to the roads and protection to the caravans, and the friend of all Franks who deserve your friendship.' 'And you,' said he, laughing, 'what will you say of me?' 'I shall say', replied I, 'what I have seen; that you are as powerful and as hospitable as a prince of the Franks; that you have been calumnated; and that you deserve the friendship of all Europeans, who like me, have experienced your kindness and the protection of your sabre.' Abou Gosh appeared enchanted....

Abou Gosh is the actual sovereign of about 40,000 Arabs of the mountains of Judea, from Ramlah to Jerusalem, from Hebron to the mountains of Jericho. This sovereignty, which has descended in his family for some generations, has no other foundation than his own power. In Arabia, they do not discuss the origin or the legitimacy of power: it is acknowledged, it is submitted to so long as it exists.

A family is more ancient, more numerous, more rich, more brave than others; the chief of this family naturally obtains more influence over his tribe; the tribe itself is better governed, more skilfully and more valiantly commanded in war than other tribes, and without dispute becomes predominant. Thus have originated all those supremacies of chiefs and tribes which are recognized throughout Asia. Power is here formed and preserved as a part of the order of nature: it originates in family ties, and the fact of this ascendancy, once established and acknowledged, is no longer contested; obedience becomes a matter of religious and filial duty. Great events and heavy misfortunes must occur to overthrow a family; and this, as it were voluntary nobility, is preserved for centuries. One does not thoroughly understand the feudal system without having visited these Eastern countries; here may be seen the means by which, in the middle ages, all those families, all those local powers which reigned in the castles, the villages and the provinces, erected themselves into power. It is the first degree of civilization....

*The Mount of Olives*
*28 October 1832*

We had traced for a quarter of an hour this last and lugubrious avenue, when suddenly the rocks separating on both sides, left us in face of the walls of Jerusalem, to which we had come close without knowing it. A vacant space of some hundred paces alone lay between us and the gate of Bethlehem: this area, barren, sloping and waste, resembling the glacis which at a certain distance surrounds the fortified towns of Europe, opened to the right and descended with a gentle declivity into a narrow valley. To the left it bore five old trunks of olive trees, bent almost horizontally under the weight of time and the sun: trees petrified, as it were, like the barren fields from whence they have painfully issued. The gate of Bethlehem, commanded by two towers, crowned with gothic battlements, but desolate and silent as the gate of a deserted castle, stood open before us. We passed some minutes immovable, to contemplate it; our eager desire to pass it was irrepressible; but the plague was at its height in Jerusalem; and we had been received into the convent of St John the Baptist of the Desert only under the most formal promise of not entering the city. We therefore entered it not, but turning to the left, wound slowly round the long high walls, built on the edge of a deep ditch or moat, in which we occasionally distinguished the foundation stones of Herod's ancient enclosure. At every step we passed Turkish cemeteries, whitened with funeral monuments, surmounted by the turban....

... We crossed the bridge [across the Cedron] and alighted from our horses in front of a beautiful building of composite architecture, of a severe and antique character, which is nearly buried in the depth of the Valley of Gethsemane and occupies all its breadth. It is the supposed tomb of the Virgin, Mother of Christ, and belongs to the Armenians, whose convents were the chief seat of the plague. We did not, therefore, enter the sanctuary itself, and I contented myself with falling on my knees on the marble step of the court in front of this pretty temple....On rising, I observed behind me about an acre of land, touching on one side the elevated bank of the torrent of Cedron, and on the other, rising gently to the base of the Mount of Olives. A low wall of stones, without cement, surrounds this field; and eight olive trees, standing at about twenty or thirty paces distance from each other, nearly cover it with their shade. These olive trees are amongst the largest of their species I have ever seen: tradition makes their age mount to the era of the incarnate God, who is said to have chosen them to conceal His divine agonies. Their appearance might, if necessary, confirm the tradition which venerates them: their immense roots, the growth of centuries, have lifted up the earth and stones which covered them, and rising many feet above the surface of the soil, offer to the pilgrim natural benches, upon which he may kneel, or sit to collect the holy thoughts which descend from their silent heads....I separated from the caravan which had tarried round the tomb of the Virgin, and seated myself for a moment on the roots of the most solitary and oldest of these olive trees; its shade hid the walls of Jerusalem from me; and its large trunk screened me from the observation of some shepherds, who were tending black sheep on the brow of the Mount of Olives.

I had nothing within sight but the deep and rugged ravine of Cedron and the tops of other olive trees which, from this spot, cover the extent of the Valley of Jehoshaphat. No noise arose from the dry bed of the torrent; no leaf trembled on the tree; I closed my eyes for a moment and reverted in thought to that night, the eve of redemption of the human race....

I remounted my horse and turning my head every instant to see something more of the valley and the city, I climbed in a quarter of an hour the Mount of Olives; every step which my horse took in the path which leads up the Mount opened to me a new quarter or another building in Jerusalem. I reached the summit, crowned by a ruined mosque, covering the spot where our Lord ascended to Heaven after his resurrection; I declined a little to the right of this mosque to gain two broken columns lying on the ground at the foot of some olive trees, on a platform which overlooks at once Jerusalem, Zion and the valley of St Saba leading to the Dead Sea....Here I sat down, and this was the scene before me.

The Mount of Olives, on whose summit I was seated, slopes suddenly and rapidly down to the deep abyss called the Valley of Jehoshaphat, which separates it from Jerusalem. From the bottom of this sombre and narrow valley, the barren sides of which are everywhere paved with black and white stones, the funereal stones of death, rises an immense hill, with so abrupt an elevation, that it resembles a fallen rampart; no tree here strikes its roots, no moss even can fix its filaments; the slope is so steep, that the earth and stones continually roll from it and it presents to the eye only a surface of dry dust, as if powdered cinders had been thrown upon it from the heights of the city. Towards the middle of this hill, or natural rampart, rise high and strong walls of large stones, not externally sawed by the mason, which conceal their Hebrew and Roman foundations beneath the same cinders, and are here from 50 to 100, and further on from 200 to 300 feet in height. The walls are here separated by three city gates, two of which are fastened up, and the only one open before us seems as void and as desolate as if it gave entrance only to an uninhabited town. The walls rising above these gates sustain a large and vast terrace, which runs along two-thirds of the length of Jerusalem....This magnificent platform, prepared no doubt by Nature, but evidently finished by the hand of man, was the sublime pedestal upon which arose the Temple of Solomon; it now supports two Turkish mosques.... Beyond the platform, the two mosques, and the site of the Temple, the whole of Jerusalem is stretched before us, like the plan of a town in relief, spread by an artist upon a table; the eye loses not a roof or a stone. This city is not, as it has been represented, an unshapely and confused mass of ruins and ashes, over which a few Arab cottages are thrown, or a few Bedouin tents pitched; neither is it like Athens, a chaos of dust and crumbling walls, where the traveller seeks in vain the shadow of edifices, the traces of streets, the phantom of a city; but it is a city

*View of Jerusalem from the Mount of Olives, c.1870*

shining in light and colour! presenting nobly to view her intact and embattled walls, her blue mosque with its white colonnades, her thousand resplendent domes, from which the rays of the autumnal sun are reflected in a dazzling vapour; the façades of her houses, tinted by time and heat, of the yellow and golden hue of the edifices of Paestum, or of Rome; her old towers, the guardians of her walls, to which neither one stone, one loophole, nor one battlement is wanting; and, above all, amidst that ocean of houses, that cloud of little domes which cover them, is a dark elliptical dome, larger than the others, overlooked by another and a white one. These are the churches of the Holy Sepulchre and of Calvary; from hence they are confounded and appear drowned in the immense labyrinth of domes, edifices and streets, which encompass them....

The view is the most splendid that can be presented to the eye of a city that is no more; for she still seems to exist as one full of life and youth; but on contemplating the scene with more attention, we feel that it is really no more than a fair vision of the City of David and Solomon. No noise arises from her squares and streets, no roads lead to her gates from the east or from the west, from the north or from the south, except a few paths winding among the rocks, on which you meet only half-naked Arabs on their asses, some camel drivers from Damascus, or women from Bethlehem or Jericho, carrying on their heads a basket of raisins from Eingeddi, or a cage of doves, to be sold on the morrow under the the turpentine tree beside the city gates. We were seated the whole of the day before one of the principal gates; we walked round the walls; no one passed in or out; no mendicant even was seated against the curbstones; no sentinel showed himself at the threshold; we saw, indeed, no living object, heard no living sound; we found the same void, the same silence, at the entrance of a city containing 30,000 souls, during the twelve hours of the day, as we should have expected before the entombed gates of Pompeii or Herculaneum....

To the left of the platform, the Temple, and the walls of Jerusalem, the hill which supports the city suddenly sinks, stretches itself, and descends in gentle slopes, sometimes broken by terraces of rolling stones. On its summit, at some hundred paces from Jerusalem, stands a mosque, and a group of Turkish edifices, not unlike a European hamlet, crowned with its church and steeple. This is Sion! the palace, the tomb of David! the seat of his inspiration and of his joys, of his life and his repose! A spot doubly sacred to me, who have so often felt my heart touched, and my thoughts enraptured by the sweet singer of Israel! the first poet of sentiment! the king of lyrics....

I, the feeble poet of an age of silence and decay, had I domesticated at Jerusalem, I should have selected, for my residence and abiding place, precisely the spot which David chose for his at Sion. Here is the most beautiful view in all Judea, Palestine, or Galilee. To the left lies Jerusalem with its Temple and its edifices, over which the eyes of the king or of the poet might rove at large without his being seen from thence. Before him, fertile gardens descending in steep declivities, lead to the bed of that torrent, in the roar and foam of which he delighted. Lower down, the valley opens and extends itself; fig trees, pomegranates and olive trees overshadow it. On one of those rocks suspended over the rolling tide; in one of those sonorous grottoes refreshed by the breeze and by the murmur of the waters; or at the foot of a terebinthus, ancestor of that which shelters me, the divine poet doubtless awaited those inspirations which he so melodiously poured forth! And why will they not also visit me, that I might recount in song the griefs of my heart, and of the hearts of all men, in these days of perplexity, even as he sang of his hopes in an era of youth and of faith? Song, alas! no longer lives in the heart of man, for despair sings not! And until some new beam shall descend upon the obscurity of our times, terrestrial lyres will remain mute, and mankind will pass in silence from one abyss of doubt to another, having neither loved, nor prayed, nor sang.

# T.E. LAWRENCE
## 1888–1935

T.E. Lawrence by Augustus John

*Thomas Edward Lawrence was born in 1888 and educated at Jesus College, Oxford, where he became deeply interested in both archaeology and the Middle East. He studied Arabic, travelled to Syria in 1909, and from 1910 to 1914 worked on the excavation of Carchemish on the banks of the Euphrates. In 1914 he undertook an archaeological survey of southern Palestine for the Palestine Exploration Fund and, together with C.L. Woolley, made his way from Gaza to Ain Kadeis. Their description of the survey, The Wilderness of Zin, was published privately in 1915. One of its valuable features was Lawrence's account of the Ain Kadeis area and his dismissal of the prevailing view that this was the watering-place of the wandering Israelites during their forty years in the desert. During the First World War his ability to penetrate the 'closed shop' of nomadic Arab life and to win the confidence of the Arabs, enabled him to reanimate the revolt against the Turks. After the war, he spent some time as adviser to the Colonial Office, but his growing reputation as an almost mythical figure – and his inability at the Paris Peace Conference to achieve all he wanted for the Arab cause – led him to have a nervous breakdown. His account of the Arab Revolt, The Seven Pillars of Wisdom, was privately printed in 1926 and a shortened version of it, Revolt in the Desert, appeared in 1927. In 1922 he enlisted in the RAF as John Hume Ross and, a year later, joined the tank corps as T.E.Shaw. He returned to the RAF, but had retired at the time of his death in a motor-cycle accident in 1935.*

*Ain Kadeis*

Below the Negev proper, and divided from it on the west by a broad depression, is a mass of steep white hills, grouped in a cluster of peaks and ridges that have different names among the different Arab tribes, and from different sides....This chain of foothills is important geographically in that it divides two water systems. To the north of it is a running-together of wadies into a plain about Kossaima, and to the south of it is another running-together of wadies to simulate a second plain, which modern writers have called the plain of Ain Kadeis. This second plain is held in by considerable hills: on the east is Jebel el Ain, a rugged bow of cliffs in limestone and flint, with only one possible way over it; on the north is the watershed already mentioned, a procession of pointed hills; on the west and south there are no steep places, but rows of inconspicuous ridges, slowly adding up to a modest height. Looked at from these boundaries the contours of the lower ground fall flat, whereas in reality the whole surface is irregular, running up here and there into tolerable hills, and all seamed with stony torrent-beds. The soil is sandy, between stones, and there are only rare traces of ancient civilization. The Arabs – husbandmen here without hope – still plough each winter a little of the further wady beds, and in wet years reap a harvest. But Ain Kadeis is the only water in the district, and that a spring on the westward slopes of the great mountain far up the Wady Ain Kadeis.

The name Kadeis was so reminiscent of Kadesh-Barnea of the Israelites, that as soon as it was recorded of a spring it naturally loomed up in Western eyes with an importance inexplicable locally. The Arabs know nothing of a plain of Ain Kadeis: to them the name is that of a water-spring in a small valley called after it, and the great area of low land outside the mouth of the valley is not a plain at all, or connected with its tributary wady in any way by name. Yet one party of travellers after another set out, either from Syria or from Egypt, with this obscure water-hole as their avowed object. Ain Kadeis is too small to water the flocks of other than the few poor families who live near it, and, as we found, too remote from all roads to come to the notice of such Arab guides as live at any distance. But this native ignorance was interpreted as deep-seated policy, and so foreigners came to believe that the spring had remained, from the time of Moses, still a holy place (we do not really know whether even Moses thought it holy) – some great head of water in an oasis too beautiful and too precious to be disclosed to Christian eyes. Its Arabs took on a sinister character: they became by degrees inhospitable, sullen, fanatical, treacherous, bloody. And yet all the time, had the world but known it, the place had been seen, measured and described by Palmer on his visit in 1870, with his usual minute accuracy and vividness....

...The valley of Ain Kadeis is unusually naked, even among the valleys of the south country. At its mouth it is a broad, flood-torn wilderness of stone, about which a torrent-bed twists from side to side, shallow and spreading in the longer stretches, but cut twelve or fifteen feet deep through limestone shingle at the bends. In the near side of the valley are the last remains of rough terrace-walling, and near by, a little to the north of the wady entrance on the sand-hills, we found ancient remains. There were eight poor ring-graves, some sherds of Byzantine pottery, and a few rough stone foundations that might in courtesy be called a farmhouse. These late Christian remains seemed to us probably to mark the highest level of the population of old Kadeis.

After the entrance to the valley quickly draws in and becomes, if possible, more stony than before. On each side the hills are very steep and bare, and shine painfully white in the glare of the sun. There is nowhere any green place, or any smooth ground, until the actual spring is reached; instead, great polished boulders have rolled off the cliff-sides into the

*The plain of Ain Kadeis photographed by Lawrence and Woolley in 1914*

stream bed, and at times half block the water channel with their huge bulk. In and out of such as these, over small and slippery stones, up and down the steep torrent bank leads the rough track to the wells. In all its length the Wady Ain Kadeis is a most unmitigated desert.

The springs themselves are made up of two or three water-holes under a cliff. From these flow out steady trickles of water, very good and sweet ('like sugar' say the Arabs), constant throughout the winter and summer. They unite in a tiny stream which runs under the rocks, forming occasional pools, for about a hundred yards, and then comes to a stagnant and smelly end beneath a mighty boulder. The flow of water is a plentiful one for the needs of the few nomad households that now are the miserable population of the valley. Certainly they could not water there at one time all their flocks for lack of room (our men brought our camels two by two), but in this dry country the smallest running water is a precious thing, and so Wady Kadeis, in spite of its lack of pasture and of smooth ground for camping, has always two or three families living in its side-ravines, and the local Arabs have profited by the opportunity of constant water to establish a graveyard on a hillock near at hand. The goats of these Arabs, and their camels, continually driven to the well, have formed round it a patch of manure heavy enough to hide the boulders underneath, and to give root-hold to a little grass. This tiny plot, existing on sufferance of the winter floods, is the verdure that in [H.C.] Trumbull's eyes blotted out the sterile slopes around: just as the fig trees, from which his patience presently expected ripe figs, are two or three stunted roots of the uneatable wild sort, growing under cover of some larger boulders in the torrent-bed round a corner below the springs. The biggest of these bushes has old gnarled branches growing to more than a man's height, but the others are difficult to find.

Trumbull celebrates particularly the flowers of the valley, but they are only the common bloom of all the dry country, which flourish for the few days after rain till the sun's heat cuts them down. While they last, one who peers between the rocks throughout all Sinai will see a garden in what from a few feet off is blasted wilderness. Ain Kadeis, with its running water, is, of course, a little richer than most places at such times. Lastly, the pool into which Trumbull's Arabs, after stripping, plunged so rashly to have a bath, is only about a foot or eighteen inches deep, and full of very large and sharp stones....

### Kadesh-Barnea

It would perhaps be improper to close ... without any reference to the vexed question of Kadesh-Barnea. The unfortunate vagueness of the Pentateuch geographically, and its lack of synthesis historically, cause the end of all such controversies to be a deeper confusion than the beginning: therefore, so far as possible, we have kept out of our pages any reference to the barren literature of today which wrangles over indeterminable Bible sites. In most cases the strife is about a Hebrew name, and its possible reappearance in a modern Arab form. That glib catchword 'the unchanging East' has blinded writers to the continual ebb and flow of the inhabitants of the desert. It is hopeless to look for an Arab tribe which has held its present dira for more than a very few generations: and to expect continuity of a name, as in settled districts in Syria, is vanity. A second factor to be remembered is that the Jews were an unscientific people, anxious only to get through the inhospitable desert as soon as might be. Research into local nomenclature is today very difficult among the tribesmen; and it is not likely that Moses was more patient and painstaking than a modern surveyor. Probably, as often as not, the Israelites named for themselves their own camps, or unconsciously confounded a native name in their carelessness.

At the same time, by good or ill fortune, the problem of Kadesh-Barnea is a little narrower and little more documented than most. We are told that the Jews left Ezion-Geber and went to the Wilderness of Zin, which is Kadesh; and that the latter touched on the boundaries of Edom. We know where Ezion-Geber was, more or less, and where Edom was; though not the faintest light upon her boundaries. Somewhere between these points the children of Israel seem to have spent nearly forty years. We have no safe clue as to the numbers of the tribes, nor do we know their social condition; and this capital ignorance qualifies all discussion as to how they were disposed. There must, however, have been at least some thousands of them. They must have been genuine nomads, scattering to all corners of the desert in groups of two or three tents, in which case Moses was an even better organizer than we knew, to gather his people again and launch them against Palestine as a disciplined army; or they may have been a tribal group keeping to one district and moving a mile or two in this direction or in that as they devoured the pasture. If this second view be accepted, then it is definitely our opinion that only in the Kossaima district are to be found enough water and green stuffs to maintain so large a tribe for so long, and that therefore the

Wilderness of Zin and Kadesh-Barnea must be the country of Ain el Guderat, Kossaima, Muweillah and Ain Kadeis. The similarity between the names Kadeis and Kadesh need not be a mere coincidence, for the former is just as likely to be of ancient as of recent origin. The extension by the Israelites of what is now the name of a small isolated valley to a whole district can be explained by the fact that travellers coming from Akaba would happen first on the low country at that valley's mouth, a country less detectable than the wastes they had just left, and might easily, as strangers, call the whole plain after their first watering-place. On the other hand, the assumption, necessary to our minds, that the place-name was extended to a district embracing other and better water-holes, undermines the identification of Ain Kadeis valley as the scene of events related as happening at Kadesh. These may have taken place anywhere in the Kossaima neighbourhood. We are told that at one well in Kadesh the Israelites found the water insufficient – and if there were more than twenty families of them, and the spring were the present Ain Kadeis, then their complaints must be considered moderate. Thereupon Moses produced the water of Meribah, so called to distinguish it from the first well. Certainly it is useless to look for this copious fount in the barren gorge of Ain Kadeis unless we suppose that it dried up as miraculously as it appeared....

Strategically the Kossaima district agrees well with what we know of Kadesh-Barnea. The Darb el Shur, the road of their forefathers, stretching westwards before the eyes of the mutinous Israelites, suggested an easy return to Egypt; the same road runs northwards to Hebron, whither the spies went up to view the Land of Promise. From the south runs up the main road from Elath, one of the stations on the Exodus route. Westwards there is a choice of roads.... These roads running out to north, south, east and west – all directions in which journeys were planned or made from Kadesh-Barnea – together with its abundance of water and wide stretch of tolerable soil, distinguish the Kossaima plain from any other district in the Southern Desert, and may well mark it out as the headquarters of the Israelites during their forty years of discipline.

# EDWARD LEAR

## ◄ 1812–88 ►

*Edward Lear, 1840 (portrait by Wilhelm Marstrand)*

*Edward Lear was born in London on 12 May 1812. As part of a large family, he was forced to earn his living at the age of fifteen and was employed as a draughtsman in the gardens of the Royal Zoological Society. In 1832 he published one of the earliest volumes of large-scale, coloured plates of birds in England,* The Family of the Psittacidae. *In 1832 he came under the patronage of Lord Derby and was employed at his residence, Knowlsley. Lear drew the plates to* The Knowlsley Menagerie, *and invented for his patron's grandchildren his famous* Book of Nonsense, *which was later published in 1846. In 1837, partly for health reasons, he left England and never again resided permanently in his native country. For several years he lived in Rome and wandered as a sketcher through many parts of southern Europe. In the spring of 1858 he visited Syria and Palestine and, in pursuance of a long-cherished wish, arranged a visit to Petra, the unique rock city of Edom, so vividly recounted below. Lear was accompanied on his journey to Petra by his faithful Suliot servant, Giorgio, who had attached himself to his master while Lear was living in Corfu and roaming over the wilds of Albania. The following account, taken from one of his unpublished journals, first appeared in* Macmillan's Magazine *in 1897. He later published several lively books about his travels, the best-known being* Journal of a Landscape Painter in Greece and Albania *(1851) and* Journal of a Landscape Painter in Corsica *(1870). He had an insatiable love of travel and, even at the age of sixty, embarked on a long tour of most of the Indian empire. Lear called* himself a topographical artist and he exhibited many of his paintings at the Royal Academy from 1850 to 1873. In 1871 he settled in San Remo, where he spent the rest of his life. His posthumous reputation as a water-colourist has steadily grown, but he is best remembered for his incomparable books of nonsense verse, with their linguistic fantasies, humour and imaginativeness.

*A Leaf from the Journals of a Landscape Painter*
*Hebron, 7 April 1858*

In came my dragoman Abdel with various Arabs, and lastly no less a person than the Sheikh of the Jelaheen himself....A child might have read the old Arab's face , which was expressive of an amount of cunning and avarice hardly to be exceeded in one man's countenance. Abdel says, beamingly, that he has made a compact with the sheikh that I shall go with an escort of fifteen to Petra, to remain there a week and to return by the Dead Sea, where I am to remain four days ... for the sum of £30, which is to include the expense of camels and all etc.

This arrangement will give me ample time for what I wish to draw; but it is more expensive than I like, and it may be in practice far less agreeable than in theory, seeing that the trustworthiness of the Jelaheen has to be proved. Yet it suits me better to close than to remain in Hebron bargaining for better terms....So I agree to the plan, and half the money is as usual to be paid beforehand....

*9 April:* We are all moving long before daybreak. Myriads of gay little grasshoppers jump up like spray from the grass at each footfall as I walk. The camels appear good, a matter of great import for such a journey. Mine is a very handsome and young one, and behaves himself tranquilly. Giorgio's looks as if he had been boiled or shaved, but is spare and active. Then there is a huge white Hubblebubble who is evidently a pièce de résistance for all the goods the others decline to carry; one for Abdel, one for the Sheikh Salah [the chief guide] and one more for luggage, complete the tale of six. But this last individual turns out to be a violent party and refuses to be loaded, particularly opposing all attempts to make him carry the cage of poultry, as an uncamel-like and undignified burden. Altogether the din of snarling, growling, screaming and guggling was considerable; and the lean Jehaleen attendants, of whom there are fifteen, seem a very filthy and incapable lot by way of escort. But it is useless to complain; the Petra journey is to be made now, so be it made as best it may.

At length we started. A walk over the South Downs from Lewes to Brighton would give a fairly correct idea of the general forms of the rolling hill scenery intersected with smooth dales, through which we passed; but here there is much more rock and much less verdure, though certain portions of the land are pretty profusely tufted with herbs. I always hate camel-riding and walked on for more than an hour, finding a constant pleasure in the exquisite carpets of lilac hepatica and pale asphodel spread over the most level ground, and the knots of sage, broom and other shrubs which vary the hill-sides....

*10 April:* What a strange calm world was the tawny hollow glen landscape, dusky-tufted and be-camelled with ghostly wanderers, before the sunlight came gloriously bursting over the dark sapphire heights of Moab! By sunrise all over that world is astir, and thanks to all-powerful quinine the Howadji can look forward to a good day's journey. At six-fifteen we start, an early move displeasing to the wicked camel, who said in his heart, 'Hang this! I'll stop their journey!' and forthwith beginning to dance and kick, all the baggage rolled away, and twenty minutes were used in replacing it. From the nature of the ground to be passed today, there will be plenty of walking up and down the Sufâa pass....The old Sheikh Salah, clad in a single linen garment resembling that which painters allot to the infant Samuel, and giving him the appearance of a white sack of flour, sleeps as he adheres to the inferior end of his camel, who howls and shrieks at intervals, as is the wont of some of these beasts. 'In the Arab when his camel not making the noise he is never liking him of a beast,' says the dragoman Abdel apologetically. As the heat increases with the advancing day I have to struggle hard against the irritation which riding these animals always brings me, none the less that just hereabouts they are greatly pestered with flies on their heads, as a relief from which they turn their necks quickly to bump and rub their noses on their riders' boots....

*13 April:* Clear pale sky before sunrise, with long rosy clouds floating pennon-like round the harsh jagged outline of Hor. A particularly early start was ordered, that the mountain might be ascended before the hotter part of the day; but this precautionary measure was, to say the least, modified by the wicked camel's twisting himself viciously against the first rocks he encountered, and shooting all the luggage into a deep hole below. 'I am quite sick of camels,' says the traveller in the East. So I walked onwards and upwards for four hours, glad to be away from the wearisome janglings and yells of my unpleasant suite, and longing with increasing impatience for the first glimpse of Petra's wonders. Every step opened out fresh interest and beauty in the wild scenery; immense chasms and vast views over strange boundless desert unfolded themselves at each turn of the winding path up the steep mountain; and at one spot the intensity of giant-crag solitude, deepest rifts and high pinnacles of naked rock, was more wondrous than anything I have ever seen except the sublimity of Gebel Musa and Sinai. About nine we reached the highest part of the mountain ascent, and passing the ridge immediately below the rocks of Gebel Haroun (Aaron's mountain), now upon our left, entered the first or upper part of Wady Mousa on its western side. But it was nearly another hour before, still descending by winding tracks, we reached the first cavern tombs and the first coloured rocks. The slow advance chills with a feeling of strange solitude the intruder into the loneliness of this bygone world, where on every side are tokens of older greatness, and where between then and now is no link. As the path wandered among huge crags and over broad slabs of rock, ever becoming more striped and glowing in colour, I was more and more excited with curiosity and expectation. And after passing the solitary column which stands sentinel-like over the heaps of ruin around, and reaching the open space whence the whole area of the city and the vast eastern cliff are fully seen, I own to having been more delighted and astonished than I had ever been by any spectacle. Not that at the first glance the extent and magnificence of this enchanted valley can be appreciated: this its surprising brilliancy and variety of colour, and its incredible detail, forbid. But after a while, when the eyes have taken in the undulating slopes terraced and cut and covered with immense foundations and innumerable stones, ruined temples, broken pillars and capitals, and the lengthened masses of masonry on each side of the river that runs from east to west through the whole wady, down to the very edge of the water – and when the sight has rested on the towering western cliffs below Mount Hor, crowded with perforated tombs, and on the astonishing array of wonders carved in the opposite face of the great eastern cliff – then the impression that both pen and pencil in travellers' hands have fallen infinitely short of a true portrait of Petra deepens into certainty. Nor is this the fault of either artist or author. The attraction arising from the singular mixture of architectural labour with the wildest extravagances of nature – the excessive and almost terrible feeling of loneliness in the very midst of scenes so plainly telling of a past glory and a race of days long gone – the vivid contrast of the countless fragments of ruin, basement, foundation, wall and scattered stone, with the bright green of the vegetation, and the

*The Theatre at Petra, by David Roberts*

rainbow hues of rock and cliff – the dark openings of the hollow tombs on every side – the white river-bed and its clear stream, edged with superb scarlet-tufted blossom of oleander alternating with groups of white-flowered bloom – all these combine to form a magical condensation of beauty and wonder which the ablest pen or pencil has no chance of conveying to the eye or mind. Even if all the myriad details of loveliness in colour, and all the visible witchery of wild nature and human toil could be rendered exactly, who could reproduce the dead silence and strange feeling of solitude which are among the chief characteristics of this enchanted region? What art could give the star-bright flitting of the wild dove and rock-partridge through the oleander gloom, or the sound of the clear river rushing among the ruins of the fallen city? Petra must remain a wonder which can only be understood by visiting the place itself....

... Taking with me Giorgio and the black Feragh ... I wandered on eastward through the valley, of which the spaciousness seemed to me more impressive at each step, and the mighty accumulation of ruin more extraordinary. Wonderful is the effect of the east cliff as we approach it with its colours and carved architecture, the tint of the stone being brilliant and gay beyond my anticipation. 'Oh master,' said Giorgio (who is prone to culinary similes), 'we have come into a world where everything is made of chocolate, ham, curry powder and salmon'; and the comparison was not far from an apt one. More wonderful yet is the open space, a portion of it cut out into the great theatre, from which you approach to the ravine of the Sik. Colour and detail are gorgeous and amazing beyond imagination. At length we reached the mouth of the Sik, the narrowing space between the loftier walls of rock becoming more overgrown with oleander and broom, and the ravine itself, into which you enter by a sharp turn on your right, seeming to close appallingly above your head. Not far from the entrance I turned round to see the effect of the far-famed Khasmé or rock-fane which is opposite this end of the ravine, a rose-coloured temple cut out in the side of the mountain, its lower part half hidden in scarlet blossom, and the whole fabric gleaming with intense splendour within the narrow cleft of the dark gorge, from 400 to 700 feet in height, and ten or twelve broad. I did not penetrate further into the Sik, supposing I should have ample time in the several days I had arranged to spend at Petra, and wishing as soon as possible to obtain a general view of the valley. Retracing my steps I sat down at noon to draw, and did so uninterruptedly until it grew too dark to see the marks of my pencil or the colours I was using. First promising to call the anxious Feragh if I strayed out of sight of the tents, I worked on the whole view of the valley looking eastward to the great cliff, then in the bed of the stream among its flowering shrubs, then on one of the higher terraces where a mass of fallen columns lies in profuse confusion, not unlike the ruins of the Sicilian Selinunti, and gathered scraps and coloured effects of the whole scene from various points. And lastly at sunset I turned to draw the downward stream running to the dark jaws of the western cliff, all awful in deep shadow which threw a ghastly horror over their tomb-crowded sides, above which rose the jagged summit of Mount Hor against the clear golden sky. As the sun went down, the great eastern cliff became one solid wall of fiery-red stone, rose-coloured piles of cloud resting on it and on the higher hills beyond like a new poem-world betwixt earth and heaven. Purple and darkling the shadows lengthened among the overthrown buildings and over the orange, red and chocolate rocks of the foreground, over the deep green shrubs and on the livid ashiness of the white watercourse. Silent and ghostly-terrible rose darker and darker the western cliffs and the heights of Aaron's burial-place, till the dim pale lights fading away from the myriad crags around left this strange tomb-world to death-like quiet and the grey gloom of night. Slowly I went to my tent, happy that, even if I could carry little with me as a correct remembrance of this wonderful place, I had at least seen the valley and ruins of the rock-city of Edom.

# JOHN MACGREGOR

## ◄ 1825–92 ►

*John Macgregor and the Rob Roy under siege from hostile natives on the Jordan*

*John Macgregor was born on 24 January 1825 near Edinburgh. In 1839 he went to Trinity College, Dublin, where he remained a year taking a high position in maths. He was later called to the Bar in London. He was in Paris during the 1848 revolution and, in July 1849, he started overland across Europe, travelling on to the Levant, Egypt and Palestine. In 1851 he went to Russia and worked his way southwards to Algeria and Tunis; he later travelled across America and Canada. Between 1853 and 1863 he was largely occupied in studying modes of marine propulsion and, during the summer of 1865, he launched the canoe he had designed, the Rob Roy, on the first of his many solitary cruises for which he is so well known. Starting down the Thames and round the coast to Dover, Macgregor crossed the Channel by steamer and then navigated the rivers, canals and lakes of Europe, the chief of which were the Meuse, the Rhine, the Danube, the Seine and Lakes Constance, Zurich and Lucerne. His log of the journey, A Thousand Miles in the Rob Roy Canoe, was published in 1866. Making similar trips to Norway and Sweden, the Baltic and the North Sea, he left in 1868 for the most adventurous of his voyages – through the Suez Canal and down the Red Sea to Palestine, navigating the River Jordan. He published his account of these travels, The Rob Roy on the Jordan, on his return in 1870. He frequently lectured about his travel experiences and became famous as a pioneer of canoeing in Britain. He retired to Boscombe, near Bournemouth, as a result of failing health, where he died in 1892.*

*The Sea of Galilee*

To make a complete examination of the Holy Lake along its shore was the purpose of my voyage during the next two weeks, and by method and system we at once began with the northern shore....

The canoe had skirted slowly along this shore, keeping just far enough from the edge to enable my eye to see anything like large stones or buildings under water between me and the bank, and this was the general course pursued all round the lake. For seven hours a day during seven days my sight was half below and half above the surface, scanning every object with eager patience, and few searches are more exhaustive of time, patience and energy than this, if it be done carefully. On five other days I kept to land work only, so as to be refreshed by variety. To do this in any other lake might be wearisome enough, but here on these blessed shores it was indeed a labour of love.

Thus eyeing the deep, I began to examine the ruined wall, and to probe with my paddle. Now, at least thought I, no robber can be near, and the sight below can be scanned in peace. Certainly the shores for some way inland were perfectly clear when the search began; yet just as my eye was close to the calm water, and every sound was hushed that I might drink in the pleasures of sight, a loud shout was heard close beside me, 'Ya walud!' (Holloah! you there!) and I looked up just in time to see the dark brown body of a naked man in the very act of 'taking a header' as he dashed in from the shore towards me. But my paddle was instantly in action, and when his wet head came up at my bows, the Rob Roy was backing astern full speed, and my new friend was full half a moment too late to catch hold of her, while he received ample splashing of water from my blade in his eyes. Splendidly the fellow swam, but I merely played with him and laughed at his frantic efforts and wild shouts. He paused and stared – quite at home in deep water – spouting at me a loud and voluble, indignant address, and then he retired in defeat, while I neared the shore again....

Waiting did not get rid of him, so to lose no more time I had to go on without a proper examination of the ruin below the water, and this, I think, is the only subaqueous novelty all round the lake that was not investigated well....

The Rob Roy next arrived at Tiberias, where a crowd gathered soon on the shore, and pressed so close upon me that it was with more difficulty than usual the canoe could be shouldered and carried through the narrow lanes to the locanda, a guest house, doing half duty for an hotel, when occasionally travellers are unwise enough to leave canvas homes for stone prisons. In the great arched room, whose walls were ten feet thick and scarcely lighted, the canoe lay stretched upon the floor, and her captain on a divan. Part of my tent was hung across the room to screen it a little from the women folks who came in and out, night and day, and who could now see the boat to great advantage by peeping over and under the very feeble barrier we had placed to guard our privacy. Poor bodies, they did their best in civility and activity, and so did their other permanent lodgers, whose diminutive size was made up for by their myriads of numbers, so that long before midnight I had pronounced all houses to be wretched everywhere, and this one detestable, in comparison with the cleanly comfort of a tent....

When the Rob Roy launched again from Tiberias, all the walls and house-roofs were covered with people come out to see; so she turned about also to look at the sight on shore.

The town juts out to deep water. Ugly circular towers, built lately and badly, lean here and there, with cracks through their toppling sides. The earthquake which occurred on

New Year's Day in 1837 had its centre at Jish, but, in its wide revelry, it shook these bastions of Tiberias, and one would wish that it had levelled them entirely.

One relic of the more solid past remains – a wall of blackened bevelled stone, that just tops the water for 100 yards, and still proudly testifies to the better masons of better days gone by. The south end of this wall seemed to be a little lower than the other. This might be because more stone was left upon the north; but a nearer examination showed me that three courses of stones were above the water at the north end, and only two at the south, while the line of the bevel course was inclined; so that the whole wall, unbroken, almost unshaken, had sunk down in one grand mass obliquely towards the south; while the other rude white towers built yesterday – only a few hundred years ago – have staggered, jostling one against the other, broken into melancholy wreck....

The remarkable sinking down of the south end of Tiberias is soon explained when we paddle farther south along the shore. For there, about a mile only from the town, is the famous warm bath, always supplied from the heat of Vulcan's forges, deep in the earth, and from whence has flowed for ages a hot sulphurous stream. We must recollect that the Sea of Galilee itself is in a great hollow, depressed 650 feet into the crust of the earth. The surface of the water of the lake is so·low that, if St Paul's Cathedral were set upon the shore, and Westminster Abbey on the top of the dome, the summit of this pile would still be lower than the Mediterranean Sea.

The earth's cuticle, then, above its interior fire is constitutionally thin in Galilee....Hot water pouring out thus for thousands of years has, no doubt, still further thinned the skin of earth at this place; so, when the earthquake came, probably the crazy arch of rock gave way, and giants' halls below were crushed together, and the wall of Tiberias sunk towards that side.

Glorious sunny weather soon brightened the water as the Rob Roy paddled on ... close by the pebbly shore, which here is of beautiful white. My camp was leisurely moving to Kerak, at the south end of the lake, and so there was plenty of time for a slow and careful survey of the coast under water. The ragged ones of Tiberias all rushed out to see the canoe so close; therefore, to shake them off, and to have peace for my pleasant work, I went out to sea and lolled the time away until their short patience was exhausted; then we came back to the survey....

In the hot baths I found a number of naked and moist negroes, not very inviting to bathe along. One of them was playing a flute in the water. These baths have been a hundred times described. They are rightly within our province, too, for a word or so, being water but we turn with more pleasant feelings to the cooler sparkling wavelets of the lake itself. Nothing was found under the surface here but a number of detached squared stones. A little farther on, bold cliffs descend into the water, and the road winds over their shoulders. Huge rocks, too, are in the lake just under the cliffs, and the Rob Roy had threaded among these; but nothing seemed to be there that might not be found in any other lake.

The bays along this part are, therefore, all bad for boats, until the last bay, on the south-west ... near the mound of Kerak, where an excellent beach shelves quickly to good anchorage in flat sandy gravel. There are remains of a pier at the place, and the north-west wind is powerless in this bay.

The lake narrows at its southern end, and a charming slope of green, with gentle knolls enlivening its outlines, shows where the desperate fight took place between the Jews at Taricheae and the heavy-mailed cohorts of Rome. Now the place looks peaceful enough – with the peace of desolation. Bright anemones wave in the evening breeze; red is the most frequent colour, but white ones are scattered too. In other localities there are blue anemones; and in one spot by Jordan I noticed a red, a blue and a white anemone, all three together. This conjunction is regarded as singular.

There is some traffic along the bridle-path by the lake. You meet somebody almost every quarter of an hour. My muleteers had a palaver with each of these wayfarers and showed off the Rob Roy as part of *their* property, while they praised her exploits in florid story. Then she drew to the shelving beach near Kerak, where we can lie on the shore in the sun for rest and refreshment. Here the lake banks are of red clay, and the water is shallow along a shore of black sand, curved and indented by lagoons; for here again will Jordan once more lay hold of the waters and hurry them away ... down to the dull Dead Sea.

Our camp grows up in the evening air like mushrooms in the grass, and the canoe reclines among the oleanders, and her crew under the palm tree by our tent. This is quite away from all intruders, and no dwelling is in sight but our own; so Kerak is the place for a quiet Sunday, when the beautiful lake is beside the Sacred Book, for now, indeed, we can read a pictorial Bible.

What a relief to be out of that house at Tiberias! What a delightful change to be again in a tent by the sea. Instead of the dark draughty room, with no view, no comfort, no privacy, now there is the fairest green prospect facing me as I recline; the sweetest air around, the light of heaven above, and the sentiment and romance of a wandering life for a quiet undercurrent of delicious enjoyment....

*A Storm on the Lake*

In traversing the centre of the lake, I came rather suddenly upon a novel sight. The smooth surface of the water was undulated in short sharp swells, without any wind whatever, and none for hours before. These waves were exactly east and west in the ridges, and of the form and size of 'steamboat waves' upon the Thames. They had a uniform width of fifteen feet, and my bow often dipped deep in one as my stern left the other. Perhaps the cause of this is some volcanic perturbation either of the water or of its bed below. Molyneux noticed something of the same kind in the Dead Sea, and precisely in the same direction, north and south....

The wind soon brought the ordinary waves upon the lake, and these confused the previous distinctness of this ground swell....

Great heat soon poured down from the fierce sun, and 'something', we thought, must come of this brilliant glare. Gentle zephyrs breathed from behind me; then they lulled; then other little airs fanned my cheek on the right, and then these, too, quite waned away to calm. Patches of the smooth mirror again were ruffled on our left by squalls from the north-west right ahead. But the sun killed them one after the other, and I steadily advanced – yet all the time aware that this sort of weather was not to be trusted.

Just as the Rob Roy passed below Wady Fik, a strange distant hissing sounded ahead, where we could see that a violent storm was raging. Instantly all hands were on the alert to meet it. The waves had not time to rise. The gusts had come down upon calm water, and they whisked up long wreaths of it into the sky. The sea-birds sailed with the roaring blast, which rushed on with foam and fury, but it found the Rob Roy all ataunto. This torrent of heavy cold air was pouring over the mountain crests into the deep cauldron of the lake below, a headlong flood of wind, like a waterfall into the hollow; just as is said in Luke (viii. 23) – 'there came down a storm of wind upon the lake.'

The peculiar effects of squalls among mountains are known to all who have boated much on lakes, but on the Sea of Galilee the wind has a singular force and suddenness; and this is, no doubt, because the sea is so deep in the world that the sun rarefies the air in it

*The Sea of Galilee as seen from the town of Tiberias (photo by Frank Mason Good)*

enormously, and the wind, speeding swift above a long and level plateau, gathers much force as it sweeps through flat deserts, until suddenly it meets this huge gap in the way, and it tumbles down here irresistible.

With my best efforts I could scarcely stem the force of this head-wind, though my crew was in excellent training, and my canoe in her lightest trim. But every moment lost now in getting to the cliffs for shelter would make the work afterwards ten times harder, when the sea had time to rise. By pressing onwards, then, with every nerve, and with more exertion than at any time during the cruise, we gained at last the windward shore, and here we could look with safe amazement at the scud of the gale, careering across the lake, and twisting the foam in the air as if tied in knots of spray, which sparkled in the sun like 10,000 diamonds, while the sea-birds still flew helplessly down wind....

Swift as the tempest had come down, it vanished away as swiftly, and when we turned our bow to sea again, there was only a fine fresh breeze and common waves to meet.

# MOSES MONTEFIORE

## ◄ 1784–1885 ►

*Sir Moses Montefiore, 1881 (portrait by Henry Weigall)*

*Moses Montefiore, one of the most famous Jews of the nineteenth century, was born in Leghorn, where his parents were on a visit from London. He was first apprenticed to a firm of grocers and soon became one of the twelve Jewish stockbrokers in the City of London. Married but without children, he decided to dedicate his life to the alleviation of suffering of his coreligionists. Combined with his love of travel, he journeyed throughout the world dispensing aid and acting as an unofficial ambassador on the Jews' behalf. He first visited the Holy Land in 1827 and subsequently went there seven times, the last being in 1874, when he was ninety. Petitioned by Jews for aid wherever he travelled, his reception in Jerusalem in 1839, as described by his wife below, was as honoured as that afforded to visiting royalty. In 1858 he was the first Englishman allowed to buy land in Jerusalem (described below by his secretary, Dr Loewe), on which he erected a windmill and the Touro alms houses. He was also active in public life in England, becoming Sheriff of London in 1837 and being awarded a baronetcy in 1846. Only two of his many diaries survived after his death and were published in 1890 by Dr Loewe. Fortunately some of Judith Montefiore's journals remained, including a privately printed account of their visit to the Holy Holy Land in 1838–9.*

*Reception in Jerusalem*
*7 June 1839*

Thanks to Almighty God, we rested in peace and comfort beneath our tents! At an early hour in the morning the governor, attended by his suite, and several of our brethren, came to visit us; but the fatigues of the journey and heat of the weather rendered it necessary that we should indulge till a somewhat later hour, they went away and returned at about nine o'clock....We breakfasted under an olive tree, whose branches spread sufficiently wide to shelter us from the scorching rays of the sun. Mr A-- had provided us with luxuries for the repast, which, through his kindness, consisted of apricots, oranges, cakes, fresh butter and cheese, tea and coffee. The romantic situation in which we partook of this breakfast, added in no slight degree to its relish; and our eyes felt that they could never grow weary of contemplating the Holy City, the valley and other objects, among which was the tomb of the prophetess Khouldah, enriching the sublime landscape spread before us.

The governor proposed that we should enter the city in a day or two, when he would come officially to meet us and proclaim a holiday. We are, however, strongly persuaded not to enter, cases of plague having occurred within the last few days. It is, therefore, our determination to remain in our present position on this beautiful mount [of Olives], where the finest air, the most sublime views and associations of the noblest kind unite to comfort us and elevate our thoughts....

Mr Y--, the British consul, and his lady came to see us. They are evidently very amiable persons and will afford, I trust, as much help as it lies in their power to render to the afflicted people. Mr Y-- states it at his opinion that the chief cause of the plague is extreme poverty, and Mrs Y-- told me that she had seen people eating the grass and weeds from excess hunger. These melancholy recitals furnished fresh reasons for every effort that could be made to bring the land into cultivation and afford employment to those who are at present without any regular means of support....

*8 June:* We had our chairs, carpets and umbrellas brought towards the Valley of Jehoshapat, opposite the site of the temple, near the tomb of Khouldah, and affording a distant view of the Dead Sea. The remembrance of this Sabbath morning can never be effaced. Every spot answers minutely to the descriptive language of Scripture. The walls of the temple may have yielded to the devastating arm of the conqueror; but Mount Zion itself standest for ever. Nor are there wanting objects, or circumstances, to give a present reality and vividness to the picture of past times, full of depth and power. The olive trees spread their dim grey branches, as if emblematical of hoar antiquity. The country is sad and of melancholy aspect; and every now and then rose on the air the solemn funeral chant, the mournful lament for broken ties of love and kindred!...

*11 June:* At half-past six o'clock, accompanied by one of the Hebrew inhabitants, we went on horseback to the city of David. At the entrance to the inner court we were accosted by some Turks, to whom we explained that it was our wish to see the tomb of King David. On this one of the young men shook his head and insultingly replied that we could not see it, Ibrahim Pasha having prohibited the Franks from entering the sacred vault, particularly since a European, last year, had forced open one of the gates. Dr L[oewe] indignant at this reply, put up his stick in a menacing attitude, when the others said they would call the sheikh, who immediately made his appearance, and bowing apologized for the young man, whom he called his son. He then led us up to an apartment, where there was a kind of tomb, and which he pointed out as marking the hallowed spot we sought. But considering that David was not interred in an arched building, but in a vault, we remonstrated on the deceit attempted, and returned to the inner court, when we wrote a few lines in Arabic to the governor, requesting to be favoured, if possible, with his presence there for a few moments….At length the governor made his appearance, attended by the usual escort. We stated our wishes, and with his customary pleasing and conciliating mien, asked to see Ibrahim's order, which having read, he consulted with his officers and stated the contents of the paper. We replied that it might relate to the generality of Franks, but that having, as we had, the pasha's soldiers for guides, and being known to, and protected by all the governors of Syria, it could not apply to us; still that we could not desire to act contrary to his wishes and would therefore submit to the order. He immediately replied that we should enter and that he would have the pleasure of accompanying us. Sherbet, cibouks and coffee were then served to a large circle, and the whole party were as agreeable as if nothing had happened, the sheikh himself no less so than the rest, though he had narrowly escaped a severe blow from a stone.

Some time having been passed in complimentary conversation, we at length arose, the governor leading the way and pointing for me to follow. About a dozen of the party accompanied us, and having entered a spacious vaulted chamber, painted in Turkish fashion, we saw at the further end a trellised door, and being led to the spot, we beheld through the lattice the sacred and royal deposit of the best and noblest of kings. Yes! there we contemplated the resting-place of all that was mortal of him, whom the electing wisdom of the Almighty had placed on the throne of a kingdom, which had, at first, but the Lord himself for its King...

We read in Hebrew and then translated in the presence of all a very devotional prayer. How impossible is it to describe the feelings with which we were impressed!...

*12 June:* At a quarter past three we were called, in order to commence early preparations for entering the city. The governor arrived at six o'clock, attended by his officers and suite….After some conversation, we rose to depart. M-- expressed his wish to ride his own horse, thinking that sent for him too spirited, but the governor replied that two young men were appointed to walk by his side. All the party being mounted, the governor led the way, attended by his officers. The chief of the cavalry arranged the order of march, and two soldiers with long muskets were appointed immediately to precede me. The scene produced by the descent of the Mount of Olives, passing as we were through the most romantic defiles, and with long lines of Turkish soldiers, mounted in noble Arab horses and dressed in the most costly costume, cannot be easily described. More honour, they said, could not have been paid even to a king.

We entered the city through the Gate of the Tribes. The streets were narrow and almost filled up with loose stones, and the ruins of houses which had fallen to decay. Our guards on each side were busily engaged in keeping off the people, a precaution rendered necessary to lessen the danger of contagion. Having passed through the bazaar, we entered the Jewish quarter of the town and which appeared the cleanest of any we had traversed.

The streets, every lattice, and all the tops of the houses were thronged with children and veiled females. Bands of music and choirs of singers welcomed our arrival with melodies composed for the occasion, while every now and then the loud, quick clapping of hands gave signal that the whole vast crowd of spectators was striving to give expression to popular delight. Having reached the synagogue, the governor entered with us and then said, addressing M--, he would leave us to our devotions, and that his officers should attend us when we pleased to return to our encampment. M-- was called to the Sepher and offered

*Jewish alms houses and windmill erected by Sir Moses Montefiore outside the city walls of Jerusalem*

for all our friends in England as well as for those present....Blessings were then given for M-- and me, and for the party....

On our return the streets presented the same thronged and festive appearance as before, and thousands of good wishes and prayers were presented to heaven for our peace and happiness....

*The Oriental Method of Bargaining*
*Jerusalem and Hebron 1855*

Having surmounted the difficulties and impediments which he had to encounter, Sir Moses eventually succeeded in purchasing a track of land to the west of the Holy City, adjoining the high road from Jerusalem to Hebron, in a most beautiful and salubrious locality, and within a few minutes' walk from the Jaffa and Zion Gates. [On this land the windmill and alms houses were later built.] Here a considerable number of our coreligionists and others at once found employment on the land, and in the building of the boundary wall.

Sir Moses being the first Englishman to whom the Ottoman government granted the permission to purchase land, I give some particulars connected with the transaction.

Ahhmed Aga Dizdar, who had been Governor of Jerusalem during the reign of Mohammad Ali, and who since the year 1839 had stood in friendly relations with Sir Moses, was the owner of the land in question. When Sir Moses broached the subject of the purchase to him, his answer was: 'You are my friend, my brother, the apple of my eye, take possession of it at once. This land I hold as an heirloom from my ancestors. I would not sell it to any person for thousands of pounds, but to you I give it without any money: it is yours, take possession of it.' 'I myself, my wife and children, we all are yours.' And this was his reply to Sir Moses day after day, whenever he was asked the price for which he would sell the said property.

Ultimately, after a whole day's most friendly argument, which almost exhausted all my stock of Arabic phraseology (having acted as interpreter between him and Sir Moses), he said to me: 'You are my friend, my brother; by my beard, my head, I declare this is the case. Tell Sir Moses to give me a souvenir of 1,000 pounds sterling, and we will go at once to the Ckádee.'

The moment I informed him of the Aga's price, Sir Moses lost no time and counted out 1,000 English sovereigns, did them up in a roll and proceeded to the English consulate, together with the Aga and his friends, where the sale was effected.

On our arrival at the Máhkámeh (hall of justice) to have the purchase confirmed, we found all the members of the Meglis assembled, and the judge, or Ckádee, with his secretaries, present.

Questions were put by the judge, both to the seller and the purchaser. The purchase money was counted, and the contract of sale was read aloud and witnessed by all present....

The next day we left for Hebron....Sir Moses being desirous of establishing a dispensary for the benefit of all the poor inhabitants at Hebron, he wanted to purchase the field where we were encamped, and therefore sent for the owner, who, on being informed of the object for which the purchase of his field was required, after long consideration gave the laconic reply, 'Ten purses' (equivalent to £50). Moses agreed to the price, and gave orders to have the deed of sale prepared. On the following day the owner of the field made his appearance early in the morning. We thought he came to tell us the hour when to appear before the Ckádee. To our great surprise he said, on reconsideration, he thought he could not sell the land under £500. Sir Moses would not hear of paying such an amount, and the consequence was that the poor of Hebron lost the dispensary, which it was his intention to supply with medicines in the same way as he did to the one at Jerusalem.

# LAURENCE OLIPHANT
## ◄ 1829–88 ►

Laurence Oliphant

Laurence Oliphant was born in Cape Town in 1829. At the age of nineteen he commenced that wandering, restless life which was to be his course until his death. His first works, Khatmandu (1852) and The Russian Shores of the Black Sea (1853), described some of his earliest travels. He served as secretary to Lord Elgin in Washington, Canada and China, and then went to India, where the Mutiny was at its height. For the next few years Oliphant was an observer – or participant – in many of the revolutions taking place around the world: he was associated with Garibaldi in Italy; narrowly escaped hanging in Nicaragua; scaled the walls of Tientsin; and was nearly assassinated during the Japanese attempt to exterminate foreigners at Yedo. In 1865 he returned to England and became an MP for the Stirling burghs, but was dissatisfied with his progress in Parliament. Instead he turned to writing and published a satirical novel, Piccadilly, which was very well received. His writing career foundered when he came under the influence of the American 'prophet', Thomas Lake Harris; he joined Harris's Brotherhood of New Life colony in New York State, where he stayed until 1882. Fascinated by the idea of colonization, especially in Palestine, Oliphant and his wife then founded a community for Jewish immigrants in Haifa. In his book, The Land of Gilead (1881), he proposed the formation of a colony on the east bank of the River Jordan, and soon developed into an unofficial overlord of the colonies being founded in Palestine at the time. His experiences of some of these colonies and his travels around the country were recounted in his book, Haifa, or Life in Modern Palestine (1887), from which the following extracts are taken. Oliphant finally returned to England in 1888 and died there soon afterwards.

[93]

*A Jewish Colony in its Infancy*

About sixteen miles to the south of the projecting point of Carmel, upon which the celebrated monastery is perched above the sea, there lies a tract of land which has suddenly acquired an interest owing to the fact of its having been purchased by the Central Jewish Colonization Society of Romania, with a view of placing upon it emigrants of the Hebrew persuasion who have been compelled to quit the country of their adoption in consequence of the legal disabilities to which they are subjected in it, and who have determined upon making a bona-fide attempt to change the habits of their lives and engage in agricultural pursuits. I was invited by the local agent in charge of this enterprise to accompany him on a visit to the new property....

The experiment of associating Jews and Moslem fellahin in field labour will be an interesting one to watch, and the preliminary discussions on the subject were more picturesque than satisfactory. The meeting took place in the storehouse, where Jews and Arabs squatted promiscuously amid the heaps of grain, and chaffered over the terms of their mutual co-partnership. It would be difficult to imagine anything more utterly incongruous than the spectacle thus presented – the stalwart fellahin, with their wild, shaggy, black beards, the brass hilts of their pistols projecting from their waistbands, their tasselled kufeyiahs drawn tightly over their heads and girdled with coarse cords, their loose, flowing abbas and sturdy bare legs and feet; and the ringleted, effeminate-looking Jews, in caftans reaching almost to their ankles, as oily as their red or sandy locks, or the expression of their countenances – the former inured to hard labour on the burning hills of Palestine, the latter fresh from the ghetto of some Romanian town, unaccustomed to any other description of exercise than that of their wits, but already quite convinced that they knew more about agriculture than the people of the country, full of suspicion of all advice tendered to them and animated by a pleasing self-confidence which I fear the first practical experience will rudely belie. In strange contrast with these Romanian Jews was the Arab Jew who acted as interpreter – a stout, handsome man, in oriental garb, as unlike his European coreligionists as the fellahin themselves. My friend and myself, in the ordinary costume of the British or American tourist, completed the party.

The discussion was protracted beyond midnight – the native peasants screaming in Arabic, the Romanian Israelites endeavouring to out-talk them in German jargon, the interpreter vainly trying to make himself heard, everybody at cross-purposes because no one was patient enough to listen till another had finished, or modest enough to wish to hear anybody speak but himself. Tired out, I curled myself on an Arab coverlet, which seemed principally stuffed with fleas, but sought repose in vain. At last a final rupture was arrived at, and the fellahin left us, quivering with indignation at the terms proposed by the newcomers. Sleep brought better counsel to both sides, and an arrangement was finally arrived at next morning which I am afraid has only to be put into operation to fail signally. There is nothing more simple than farming in co-operation with the fellahin of Palestine if you go the right way to work about it, and nothing more hopeless if attempted upon a system to which they are unaccustomed. Probably, after a considerable loss of time, money and especially of temper, a more practical modus operandi will be arrived at. I am bound to say that I did not discover any aversion on the part of the Moslem fellahin to the proprietorship by Israelites of their land, on religious grounds. The only difficulty lay in the division of labour and of profit, where the owners of the land were entirely ignorant of agriculture, and therefore dependent on the co-operation of the peasants, on terms to be decided between them.

*Safed*

Next to Jerusalem, the city most highly venerated by the Jews in Palestine is Safed. I had occasion to visit it a few weeks ago on my way to a colony of Russian and Romanian Jews which has been established in the neighbourhood. Perched on the summit of a mountain nearly 3,000 feet high, it is one of the most picturesquely situated towns in the country; and there is a tradition to the effect that it was alluded to by Christ as 'the city that is set on a hill, and cannot be hid', when he preached the Sermon on the Mount, the mount being supposed to be one of the Horns of Hattin, a remarkably shaped hill.

The whole of this district is indeed full of romantic scenery. It is a country of wild gorges and huge precipices, which escape the attention of the traveller following the beaten routes, and to most of them associations are attached, investing them with an interest beyond that of a mere scenic character....

However prepossessing Safed may look from a distance, it does not bear a close acquaintance. Down the centre of every street runs an open sewer, which renders it the most odiferous and pestiferous place that it has ever been my fate to sleep in. The aspect of the population is in keeping with the general smell. One seems transported into the ghetto of some Romanian or Russian town, with a few Eastern disagreeables added. The population here have not adopted the oriental costume as they have at Tiberias, but wear the high hats, greasy gabardines and ear-curls of the Jews of Europe. Instead of Arabic, one hears nothing in the streets but 'jargon', as the dialect used by the Jews in Eastern Europe is called....

As there is nothing approaching to a hotel or boarding-house in the place, I was of course dependent on the native hospitality for board and lodging, and thus able to acquire an insight into the mode of life of rather a curious section of the human family. The majority of the Jews here are supported by a charitable fund called the Haluka, which is subscribed to by pious Jews all over the world as a sacred duty, for the purpose of providing support to those of their coreligionists who come here or to Jerusalem to pass the last years of their lives in devotional exercises, and to die on the sacred soil. The practical result of this system is to maintain in idleness and mendicancy a set of useless bigots, who combine superstitious observance with immoral practice, and who, as a rule, are opposed to every project which has for its object the real progress of the Jewish nation. Hence they regard with alarm the establishment of agricultural colonies, or the inauguration of an era of any kind of labour by Jews in Palestine. They are bitterly hostile to schools in which any secular teaching is carried on, and agree with those Western Jews who consider that any scheme for developing the material resources of Palestine by means of Jewish industry is fantastic and visionary. It is due to the Jewish population of Safed to say that this spirit does not prevail among the younger members of it. There are about 100 young Safed Jews who actually work as day-labourers on the farms of Moslems and Christians, and I was informed by one of the most liberal of the rabbis, the only one, in fact, who was inclined to promote Jewish agriculture, that about 200 families in Safed were desirous of being established on farms, while several had owned land and cultivated it, and only abandoned it at last for want of protection against the extortionate demands of Turkish tax-gatherers....

*An Ancient Jewish Community*

In one of the most remote and secluded valleys in the mountains of northern Galilee lies a village, the small population of which possesses an interest altogether unique. As I looked

*Safed, showing the Jewish quarter on the western and north-western side of the hill, just below the castle, c. 1885*

down upon it from the precipitous and dangerous path by means of which I was skirting the flank of the mountain, I thought I had rarely seen a spot of such ideal beauty. It was an oasis, not actually in a desert – for the rocky mountain ranges were covered with wild herbage – but in a savage wilderness of desolation, in the midst of which the village nestled in a forest of orange, almond, fig and pomegranate trees, the tiny rills of water by which they were irrigated glistening like silver threads in the sunlight, and the yellow crops beyond contrasting with the dull green of the hill verdure, long deprived of water, and the grey rocks which reared their craggy pinnacles above it.

The name of this village was Bukeia. I had heard vaguely of the existence of a spot in Galilee where a community of Jews lived who claimed to be the descendants of families who had tilled the land in this same locality prior to the destruction of Jerusalem and the subsequent dispersion of the race; as it had never been suspected that any remnant of the nation had clung to the soil of their fathers from time immemorial, and as it is certain that this is the only remnant that has, I took some trouble to ascertain the name of the village, and felt that it was worth a pilgrimage to visit it....

But the village does not consist altogether of Jews. In fact, they form the minority of the population, which is composed of eighty Druse, forty Greek-Christian and twenty Jewish families, the latter numbering about 120 souls in all. Refusing the invitation of the Druse and Christian sheikhs to accept their hospitality, I listened rather to the solicitations of the elderly Hebrew who eagerly placed his house at my disposal, and was the patriarch of his coreligionists, his local title being, like those of the other communities, that of sheikh. His house was a stone erection with a courtyard and contained a single large room, which, as is common in Arab houses, afforded eating and sleeping accommodation for the whole family. On this occasion it soon became crowded to excess.

First appeared the Druse sheikh, with white turban, and composed and dignified bearing. Then the sheikh of the Christians, a man in no way to be distinguished from the ordinary type of native fellahin; then the Greek priest, in his high, round-topped black hat and long black coat, reaching nearly to his feet; then the Jewish rabbi, who officiates at the synagogue, in flowing Eastern robe; then some village notables of all three religions, who all squatted on mats, forming a semicircle, of which my friends and I were the centre, and which involved a large demand upon our host for coffee, for on these occasions it is a great breach of politeness to furnish all the uninvited guests who flock in to see distinguished strangers with that invariable beverage. When one or two Moslems, who were temporary visitors to the village, dropped in from curiosity, I could not fail to be struck with the singular ethnological and theological compound by which I was surrounded. Here, in these Christian and Moslem peasants, were the descendants of those ancient Canaanites whom the conquering Jews failed to drive out of the country during the entire period of their occupation of it, though they doubtless served their conquerors as hewers of wood and drawers of water, and as farm-servants generally; for the result of the most recent and exhaustive research proves, I think, incontestably that the fellahin of Palestine, taken as a whole, are the modern representatives of those old tribes which the Israelites found settled in the country, such as the Canaanites, Hivites, Jebusites, Amorites, Philistines, Edomites....

Such were the mixed religious and race conditions by which I was surrounded, and I was much struck by the apparent tolerance and amiability with which all the members of these different religions regarded each other. The Jewish rabbi told me privately that he much preferred Druses to Christians; but he lived on good terms with all. And when I went to see the synagogue the Greek priest strolled round with me, and the rabbi returned the compliment by accompanying us when I went to visit the little Greek church. Meantime, the Hebrew sheikh had summoned all the Jewish population, and they came trooping in to perform the usual Eastern salutation of kissing the hand. Old men and maidens, young men and married women and children, I saw them all, nor, so far as dress and facial type were concerned, was it possible to distinguish them from the fellahin of the country generally. These twenty families seemed all to have descended from one stock, they all had the same name, Cohen, and they have never intermarried either with the people of the country or even with other Jews. I afterwards had some conversation with the Christian and Druse sheikhs in regard to them. They said that formerly more of the village lands belonged to them, but owing to the wars, pestilences and other misfortunes which had overtaken the country at various times, their property had become diminished; indeed, there can be little doubt that the Druses themselves, when Fakr Eddin conquered this part of the country, appropriated some of it; so that now, so far as their worldly circumstances go, the Jews are badly off. Nevertheless they do not complain and are skilful, hard-working and persevering agriculturists, to my mind more deserving of sympathy than many of their coreligionists who have come to settle in the country as colonists, depending more upon the assistance which they derive from without than upon their own efforts. The experience and example of their coreligionists at Bukeia would make the neighbourhood of that place a desirable locality for a colony.

# EDWARD ROBINSON

## ◄ 1794–1863 ►

Edward Robinson

*Edward Robinson was born in Connecticut in April 1794, where his father was a pastor. At the age of sixteen he was apprenticed to a merchant, but eager for further education he managed to go to Hamilton College, New York, where his uncle was a professor. After graduating in 1816, he studied law for a year and then tutored in maths and Greek. In 1821 he went to Andover, Massachusetts, where he came under the influence of the distinguished Hebraist, Moses Stuart, who persuaded him to devote himself to Hebrew studies. In 1826 he went to Germany and spent four years there pursuing his studies in Gottingen, Berlin and Halle. Returning to America, he was appointed Professor Extraordinary of Biblical Literature at Andover and, in 1831, founded the American Biblical Repository. From March to July 1838 he travelled to the Holy Land and for the first time a trained scholar in historical topographical research explored Palestine, paying the most careful attention to the topography, to the correct Arabic form of place-names and to the vestiges of antiquity. In the Sinai he dismissed the commonly accepted site of Mount Sinai and in Jerusalem concluded that almost every shrine in the city was inauthentic; he discovered what was later to be known as Robinson's Arch – the remains of a structure linking the Temple Mount with the old Upper City; and was the first to explore Siloa's Brook. His Biblical Researches in Palestine, Mount Sinai and Arabia Petraea, published in 1841, established his reputation as one of the foremost geographers and biblical scholars of his time. He visited the Holy Land again in 1852 and wrote a supplementary volume in 1856. He died in New York in 1863.*

*Mount Sinai*

We ascended slowly, not failing to see the track of Mohammed's camel in the rock by the way; and reached the summit of Jebel Musa at twenty minutes past ten. Here is a small area of huge rocks, about eighty feet in diameter, highest towards the east, where is a little chapel almost in ruins, formerly divided between the Greeks and Latins; while towards the S.W. about forty feet distant stands a small ruined mosque. The summit and also the body of this part of the mountain are of coarse grey granite. On the rocks are many inscriptions in Arabic, Greek and Armenian, the work of pilgrims....

My first and predominant feeling while upon this summit was that of disappointment. Although from our examination of the plain er-Râhah below, and its correspondence to the scriptural narrative, we had arrived at the general conviction that the people of Israel must have been collected on it to receive the law; yet we still had cherished a lingering hope or feeling that there might after all be some foundation for the long series of monkish tradition, which for at least fifteen centuries has pointed out the summit on which we now stood as the spot where the ten commandments were so awfully proclaimed. But scriptural narrative and monkish tradition are very different things; and while the former has a distinctness and definiteness, which through all our journeyings rendered the Bible our best guide-book, we found the latter not less usually and almost regularly to be but a baseless fabric. In the present case, there is not the slightest reason for supposing that Moses had anything to do with the summit which now bears his name. It is three miles distant from the plain on which the Israelites must have stood; and hidden from it by the intervening peaks of the modern Horeb. No part of the plain is visible from the summit; nor are the bottoms of the adjacent valleys; nor is any spot to be seen around it, where the people could have been assembled....

We determined to scale the almost inaccessible peak of es-Sufsâfeh before us, in order to look out upon the plain and judge for ourselves as to the adaptedness of this part of the mount to the circumstances of the scriptural history. This cliff rises some 500 feet above the basin; and the distance to the summit is more than half a mile. We first attempted to climb the side in a direct course; but found the rock so smooth and precipitous that after some falls and more exposures, we were obliged to give it up, and clamber upwards along a steep ravine by a more northern and circuitous course. From the head of this ravine, we were able to climb around the face of the northern precipice and reach the top, along the deep hollows worn in the granite by the weather during the lapse of ages, which give to this part, as seen from below, the appearance of architectural ornament.

The extreme difficulty and even danger of the ascent was well rewarded by the prospect that now opened before us. The whole plain er-Râhah lay spread out beneath our feet, with the adjacent wadies and mountains; while Wady esh-Sheikh on the right, and the recess on the left, both connected with, and opening broadly from er-Râhah, presented an area which serves nearly to double that of the plain. Our conviction was strengthened that here or on some one of the adjacent cliffs was the spot, where the Lord 'descended in fire' and proclaimed the law. Here lay the plain where the whole congregation might be assembled; here was the mount that could be approached and touched, if not forbidden; and here the mountain brow, where alone the lightnings and the thick cloud would be visible, and the thunders and the voice of the trump be heard, when the Lord 'came down in the sight of all the people upon Mount Sinai'. We gave ourselves up to the impressions of the awful scene; and read with a feeling that will never be forgotten the sublime account of the transaction and the commandments there promulgated ... by the great Hebrew legislator.

*Robinson's Arch, Jerusalem*

Allusion has already been made to the immense size of the stones, which compose in part the external walls of the enclosure of the mosque [of el-Aksa]. The upper part of these walls is obviously of modern origin; but to the most casual observer it cannot be less obvious that these huge blocks, which appear only in portions of the lower part, are to be referred to an earlier date. The appearance of the walls in almost every part seems to indicate that they have been built up on ancient foundations; as if an ancient and far more massive wall had been thrown down, and in later times a new one erected upon its remains....

It is not, however, the great size of these stones alone which arrests the attention of the beholder; but the manner in which they are hewn gives them also a peculiar character. In common parlance they are said to be bevelled; which here means that after the whole face has first been hewn and squared, a narrow strip along the edges is cut down a quarter or half an inch lower than the rest of the surface. When these bevelled stones are laid up in a wall, the face of it of course exhibits lines or grooves formed by these depressed edges at their junction, marking more distinctly the elevation of the different courses, as well as the length of the stones of which they are composed....

At the first view of these walls, I was led to the persuasion that the lower portions had belonged to the ancient temple; and every subsequent visit only served to strengthen this conviction. The size of the stones and the heterogeneous character of the walls render it a matter beyond all doubt, that the former were never laid in their present places by the Mohammedans; and the peculiar form in which they are hewn does not properly belong, so far as I know, either to Saracenic or to Roman architecture. Indeed, everything seems to point to a Jewish origin; and a discovery which we made in the course of our examination reduces this hypothesis to an absolute certainty.

I have already related ... that during our first visit to the S.W. corner of the area of the mosque we observed several of the large stones jutting out from the western wall, which at first sight seemed to be the effect of a bursting of the wall from some mighty shock or earthquake. We paid little regard to this at the moment, our attention being engrossed by other objects; but on mentioning the fact not long after in a circle of our friends, we found that they also had noticed it; and the remark was incidentally dropped that the stones had the appearance of having once belonged to a large arch. At this remark a train of thought flashed upon my mind, which I hardly dared to follow out, until I had again repaired to the spot, in order to satisfy myself with my own eyes, as to the truth or falsehood of the suggestion. I found it even so! The courses of these immense stones, which seemed at first to have sprung out from their places in the wall in consequence of some enormous violence, occupy nevertheless their original position; their external surface is hewn to a regular curve; and being fitted one upon another, they form the commencement or foot of an immense arch, which once sprung out from this western wall in a direction towards Mount Zion, across the Valley of the Tyropoeon. This arch could only have belonged to the bridge, which according to Josephus led from this part of the temple to the Xystus on Zion; and it proves incontestably the antiquity of that portion of the wall from which it springs....

The existence of these remains of the ancient bridge seems to remove all doubt as to the identity of this part of the enclosure of the mosque with that of the ancient temple. How they can have remained for so many ages unseen or unnoticed by any writer or traveller is a problem which I would not undertake fully to solve. One cause has probably been the

*Robinson's Arch, c.1853 (photo by James Graham)*

general oblivion, or want of knowledge, that any such bridge ever existed. It is mentioned by no writer but Josephus.…Another cause which has operated in the case of later travellers is probably the fact that the spot is approached only through narrow and crooked lanes, in a part of the city whither their monastic guides did not care to accompany them; and which they themselves could not well, nor perhaps safely, explore alone. Or if any have penetrated to the place, and perhaps noticed these large stones springing from the wall, they have probably (as I did at first) regarded their appearance as accidental, and have passed on without further examination.

*The Fountains of the Virgin and of Siloam*

We found it to be the current belief at Jerusalem, both among natives and foreigners, that a passage existed quite through between the two fountains [of the Virgin and of Siloam]; but no one had himself explored it, or could give any definite information respecting it. We therefore determined to examine it ourselves, should a fit opportunity occur. Repairing one afternoon (27 April) to Siloam, in order to measure the reservoir, we found no person there; and the water in the basin being low, we embraced this opportunity for accomplishing our purpose. Stripping off our shoes and stockings and rolling our garments above our knees, we entered with our lights and measuring tapes in our hands. The water was low, nowhere over a foot in depth, and for the most part not more than three or four inches, with hardly a perceptible current. The bottom is everywhere covered with sand, brought in by the waters. The passage is cut wholly through the solid rock, everywhere about two feet wide....At the end of 800 feet, it became so low that we could advance no further without crawling on all fours and bringing our bodies close to the water. As we were not prepared for this, we thought it better to retreat and try again another day from the other end. Tracing therefore upon the roof with the smoke of our candles the initials of our names and the figures 800, as a mark of our progress on this side, we returned with our clothes somewhat wet and soiled.

It was not until three days afterwards that we were able to complete our examination and measurement of the passage. We went now to the Fountain of the Virgin; and having measured the external distance (1,100 feet) down to the point east of Siloam, we concluded that as we had already entered 800 feet from the lower end, there could now remain not over 300 or 400 feet to be explored. We found the end of the passage at the upper fountain rudely built up with small loose stones, in order to retain the water at a greater depth in the excavated basin. Having caused our servants to clear away these stones, and having clothed (or rather unclothed) ourselves simply in a pair of wide Arab drawers, we entered and crawled on, hoping soon to arrive at the point which we had reached from the other fountain. The passage here is in general much lower than at the other end; most of the way we could indeed advance upon our hands and knees; yet in several places we could only get forward by lying at full length and dragging ourselves along on our elbows.

The sand at the bottom has probably a considerable depth, thus filling up the canal in part; for otherwise it is inconceivable how the passage could ever have been thus cut through the solid rock. At any rate, only a single person could have wrought in it at a time; and it must have been the labour of many years. There are here many turns and zigzags....The way seemed interminably long; and we were for a time suspicious that we had fallen upon a passage different from that which we had before entered. But at length, after having measured 950 feet, we arrived at our former mark of 800 feet traced with smoke upon the ceiling. This makes the whole length of the passage to be 1,750 feet; or several hundred feet greater than the direct distance externally – a result scarcely conceivable, although the passage is very winding. We came out again at the fountain of Siloam....

The purpose for which this difficult work was undertaken, it is not easy to discover. The upper basin must obviously have been excavated at an earlier period than the lower; and there must have been something to be gained, by thus carrying its waters through the solid rock into the Valley of the Tyropoeon. If the object had been merely to irrigate the gardens which lay in that quarter, this might have been accomplished with far less difficulty and expense, by conducting the water around upon the outside of the hill. But the whole looks as if the advantage of a fortified city had been taken into the account; and as if it had been important to carry this water from one point to the other in such a way, that it could not be cut off by a besieging army. Now as this purpose would have been futile, had either of these points lain without the ancient fortifications; this circumstance furnishes additional argument to show that the ancient wall probably ran along the Valley of Jehoshaphat, or at least descended to it, and included both Siloam and this upper fountain; which then either constituted or supplied the 'King's Pool', or 'Pool of Solomon'.

*The pool of Siloam (photo by Francis Frith)*

The water in both these fountains, then, is the same; notwithstanding travellers have pronounced that of Siloam to be bad, and that of the upper fountain to be good. We drank of it often in both places. It has a peculiar taste, sweetish and very slightly brackish, but not at all disagreeable....

# CROWN PRINCE RUDOLPH OF AUSTRIA

## 1858–89

*Crown Prince Rudolph of Austria*

*Born on 21 August 1858 near Vienna, the only son of Emperor Francis Joseph, Crown Prince Rudolph was heir to the Austro-Hungarian throne. Great hopes were centred on the young prince and, although his father was chiefly intent upon his military education, Rudolph's own interests lay in natural history and literature. The monumental description of the Austro-Hungarian monarchy, Oesterreich-Ungarn in Wort und Bild, was his conception and in part his work. He also wrote a number of minor books of his own, including an account of his journey to the East, including visits to Egypt and the Holy Land, Travels in the East, published in English in 1884. He became known as a free-thinker, and even a revolutionary, and he made no secret of his opposition to Austria's conservative nobility and church. As a result he drifted into increasing conflict with his father, who soon excluded him from any participation in government. His life came to a tragic end when his body, and that of his mistress, Baroness Mary Vetsera, was found at the Imperial hunting lodge of Mayerling in 1889. Numerous rumours arose connecting a series of political and clerical conspiracies with the deaths, but it is generally accepted that the Crown Prince shot his lover and afterwards committed suicide in a fit of despair, partly due to his father's order to break off the liaison.*

*Entry into Jerusalem*

We have climbed the hill – the bare desolate plateau of Jerusalem stretches before us, and in the distance rise the blue-grey mountains of the valley of the Jordan. Yellow grey is the pervading tone of the landscape, barrenness its note. The first signs of Jerusalem were visible – the great mass of the Russian church with its five cupolas, the Mount of Olives, and to the right the Greek Convent of the Crucifixion. The Holy City itself we could not yet see.

On the road there was a great triumphal arch with a Hungarian inscription. The Jewish colony stood beside with banners, singing the national hymn. With many compliments and the usual talk and noise the patriotic Jews surrounded us. They were genuine Israelites from the north of Hungary. They wore the caftan, high boots, the velvet cap, the curled beard and the accustomed ringlets. You might have supposed you were in a Carpathian village.

The whole Jewish community followed us from this point as a matter of course. Both sides of the road were already thronged with people. Jews of all countries, Christians from Asia Minor, Greeks, European pilgrims, oriental Christian women, some partly and some not at all veiled, in most picturesque costumes only to be likened to those of Hebrew women of old, very Madonnas in form and figure; beside them Copts, English tourists with their exterior so destructive of all poetry, Mohammedan country people, crippled beggars and an indescribable medley from the very ends of the earth all these idly loitering in the streets and looking curiously at us.

The procession stood drawn up, awaiting our arrival, at the point from which one first beholds Jerusalem. Everyone knelt to pray with bared head....

Some kavasses from the consulate, in peculiar theatrical costumes, rode in front with long staves. Next came a battalion of Turkish infantry with their band – wonderful combination, a procession into Jerusalem with Turkish music, and flying colours with the silver crescent! We came next in full uniform, riding, surrounded by ecclesiastics, officers of the consulates, Turkish and Christian dignitaries.

Crowds filled both sides of the streets. The road led past a large building in which the Russian pilgrims are lodged.... Two thousand of them were present on this occasion. They stood in groups looking at us. Beside the peasant of Russia itself, with his wide blouse and girdle, his knee-breeches, high boots and peculiar cylinder hat, his snub nose, blonde beard, limp greasy long hair, and unmistakable air of the northern Slavonian, one saw figures in light military cloaks, decorated with medals. There were also swarms of priests, the blonde Russian, the genuine dark Greek and the South Slavonian.

We rode through this most interesting crowd till at length we reached the Gate of Jaffa, where we dismounted and passed through the old grey gate into the interior of the Holy City.

Here stood the Latin patriarch surrounded by an extraordinarily large body of secular clergy, alumni and monks, all robed and holding lighted tapers. The patriarch and his subordinates wore beards like all Latin priests in the East.

We knelt and kissed the ground. After a short prayer the patriarch, a Genoese by birth, made an Italian address, to which I replied in French. Hereupon the priests began to sing, and advancing in pairs the procession moved slowly on. The Grand Duke and I walked to the right and left of the patriarch. All the others followed, even the Turkish dignitaries. Beside the procession marched a file of Turkish infantry....

The streets of the city are very dark and narrow. A chill vault-like air, poisoned by the most horrible smells of all kinds, pervades every spot within the confined stone walls. The pavement, consisting of irregular flags, affords the foot passengers a way of escape. Jerusalem retains unchanged the old and gloomy Hebrew character, and has nothing in common with the bright gay towns of Islam and their bazaars....

The procession went through a number of small streets, and at length reached a flight of steps. Descending these we were at the vestibule of the Church of the Sepulchre....

We now passed through some more narrow streets to the Austrian hospice, accompanied by the Turkish authorities....Immediately on our arrival we had to receive the consuls and then the Turkish authorities and the ruler of the city, all in Eastern costume, and finally the heads of all the Christian and Jewish churches. The Latin patriarch came attended by priests and monks, the Greek patriarch with his popes; then the Armenians, then Copts, and then the Syrian patriarch....

Last of all, the rabbis waited on us, their president at their head, one of the priests in the ecclesiastical hierarchy of the Hebrews of the day. This old man, with his long snowy beard, yellow waxen complexion, and fine features, was born in Spain, and wore, like most of the rabbis residing in Palestine, the ancient Hebrew dress, the coloured full overcoat trimmed with fur, the turban, a long robe and yellow slippers. I have always imagined that the Pharisees must have looked like these rabbis.

After all these most interesting visitors had left us, we quitted the hospice by a street leading to the old Gate of Damascus. Our handsome camp had been pitched just without the gate, beside some stony places and heaps of ruin, and amongst stunted olive gardens. The horses and beasts of burden lay close by. Our people slept on the ground....

After the heat and fatigue of the day rest was welcome. A cool evening and fine sunset were restorative, and when dinner was over stillness soon reigned in the camp. The incessant howling of the half-savage dogs within the walls still resounded in our ears, as well as the cries of the multitudes of jackals who hung about the slaughter-yards, which were only separated from the camp by a small valley.

*Hunting in the Jordan Valley*

Salim, the leader of a body of hunting Bedouins, was to direct us to a spot rich in game. He was a capable, excellent fellow, to whom I soon grew attached, and whom I valued as a sportsman. Bred up on horseback hunting or in battle, he might be taken as the model of a typical and absolutely free Arab. His frame was small but sinewy, his countenance marked by its energetic features, its short beard and a pair of falcon eyes. His complexion was singularly dark for this district and had more the hue of the African Arab. His apparel consisted of a small turban, a white tightly girt burnous and yellow shoes, above which his skinny legs showed. He bore by way of arms a short knife in his girdle and a whip in his hand. His comrades were about fifteen in number....They were hearty, kindly fellows, devoted to the chase. The dogs followed, wolf-like beasts of no breed or race, but whose gifts we learned to appreciate....

Salim guided us at first through so-called forests. These are more truly luxuriant green meadows, and fields of wild oats, covered more or less with bushes and dwarf trees. Everything in the Valley of the Jordan is prickly. The tall grass in spring has long thorns, with barbs which fix themselves in the flesh of man and beast; every tree is beset with prickles. It may be imagined how skin and clothes fare, and the really cruel sufferings which the sport-loving traveller in those regions must endure with resignation.

In tree and bush there was the stir of many kinds of birds. In this happy tract of land the

*The Crown Prince's entry into Jerusalem*

animal creation is closely packed together, and many beautiful, and to us novel, species presented themselves. The voice of the genuine Asiatic cooing dove was heard everywhere, and the tender turtle-doves flew high in the air above. The great shrike and many other song birds warbled amongst the thick shrubs, while quails rose at every step from the wild oats; birds of prey, eagles, kites and falcons also abounded. The smaller animals appeared to be amply represented; slender lizards, fat frogs and insects big and little made the place dangerous.

After a time we quitted this garden land and reached the steppe. Yellow grass covered the ground, reminding me vividly of home and the Hungarian marshes. Innumerable grasshoppers chirruped under our feet, and we could understand how these creatures become in Asia, at certain times, a real plague.

Suddenly Salim paused and announced that we had reached our goal. A rivulet descending from the mountain, and flowing in a direct line through the plain to the Jordan, lay before us and between us and the clay cliff....

Some of the guns were now to go to the right, others to the left or upper side of the clay bank, while the Bedouins with their dogs were to keep on the same level and beat the bushes and rocks in line. Salim remained beside me and directed the whole of the chase.

Amidst continuous howling and hurling of stones the beaters sprang and leaped about in the brook. The shots cracked merrily as one bird after another flew up, soon to fall heavily back into the bushes. Red-legged and rock partridges, quails and singing birds of many kinds flew out from their hiding-places....

We had been shooting for some time, and had gone over a considerable stretch of the bank, when suddenly the dogs gave tongue in an almost impenetrable thicket. I was searching for a rock partridge and was therefore, fortunately, at the bottom of the valley. At this moment a shot came from the other bank, and one of the gentlemen called to me that an armadillo had just been missed and was running from the dogs. The Bedouins and I followed the chase at full speed, when suddenly all was still. We found beside a tree, built up round its roots and stems, a beaver-like tower, several feet high, made out of branches. One cannot otherwise describe this admirable piece of animal architecture. On two sides there were circular entrances. When the Bedouins saw this establishment they drew back cautiously.

Salim posted me beside one entrance, while he directed his people to light a fire by the other. As the flames burnt up brightly and the building began to crackle, a peculiar creature, somewhat like a dragon, of orange colour and certainly over four feet in length, crept circumspectly out, and was going to take itself off at an easy trot, when a well-aimed shot put an end to its life. My interesting booty was a lizard. I do not know much about reptiles, but, so far as I can judge, we had one of the great Varan lizards before us.... We continued our sport, but we soon observed that the birds had been scared by the multitude of shots, and we seemed this time to have no luck with the wild boars. The entire shooting party therefore betook itself to a shady spot under a large tree, and, weary with the intense and oppressive heat, we all lay down in the grass, even the Bedouins, while their sturdy dogs panted for water with drooping tongues. There was but little water in the brook, and none that was very clear, but the excellent Achmed had, as usual, some bottles of lemonade ready, which he carried in a knapsack on his back.

After half an hour's rest Salim summoned us to further sport....Prepared for a vigorous wild boar hunt, I placed myself by a well-marked rising. The dogs had hardly got among the reeds when a wild baiting began. The sound of the chase and bay came in quick succession, and the bark of the dogs mingled with the demonaic cries of the beaters. At length, after a tedious though exciting quarter of an hour, a large wild boar rushed from the thicket and betook itself in full flight towards the point at which I stood. Deeply wounded by a shot under the shoulder, it fell as I fired, but recovering and foaming with rage, at once pursued its way. The good Achmed, not knowing the length of a wild animal's run, stood right across its path. The wounded beast came rushing on and seized the helpless man in its blind rage. By good luck I had followed as fast as I could run, and found Achmed with his knife lifted to strike and screaming loudly, standing upon one leg, while he raised the other as protection against the angry beast. The boar reared itself for the decisive onslaught, but before it could reach our hero he lay flat on the ground. Realizing his extreme danger, I fired, and the ball fortunately was instantaneously fatal. It struck the strong two-year-old female when its snout had already grasped Achmed's loose trousers. Wild boar and Egyptian now lay peacefully beside each other, the latter green from terror and trembling in every limb; it was some minutes before he recovered speech. The Bedouins, their eyes sparkling with delight, soon came on the scene. The wild boar, which is extremely like our own, especially those huge specimens from the Hungarian forests, is totally different from the much smaller, more delicately formed and pitch-black North African boar. My huntsman disembowelled the beast quickly, and the Arabs laying it on the staves which they had bound together, four men bore the heavy load back to our camp.

# LADY HESTER STANHOPE

## ◄ 1776–1839 ►

*Lady Hester Stanhope*

*Lady Hester Stanhope was born at Chevening, Kent, on 12 March 1776. In 1803 her uncle, William Pitt, asked her to keep house for him and she soon became his most trusted confidant. After his death in 1806, the king gave her a pension of £1,200. Missing the excitements of public life and mourning the deaths of her brother and of Sir John Moore, whom she loved, she decided to leave England for the Levant in 1810. She never again saw her native land. After being shipwrecked off Rhodes, she made a stately pilgrimage to Jerusalem, traversed the desert and finally settled down in 1814 among the half-savage tribes on the slopes of Mount Lebanon. Her fearlessness and charity soon caused her to be venerated as a prophetess by the tribes living around her. As time went by she adopted Eastern manners and customs, interfered in Eastern politics and held court for the many European travellers in the area. Her reckless spending led her deeper into debt so that, in 1838, Lord Palmerston felt justified in appropriating the bulk of her pension to pay off her creditors. Now poverty-stricken, Lady Hester shut herself up in her castle and lived in proud isolation until her death. Her memoirs, narrated by her physician, Meryon, were published in 1846.*

*Digging for Hidden Treasure in Ascalon, 1815*

According to a rough calculation, from the time required to make a circuit of the walls of Ascalon on horseback, its circumference is two miles. The shape is somewhat triangular, and the side towards the sea is a little longer than the others. The assertion of Strabo, that the city is built as if in a hole, and Abufelda's account that it stands on a bank, may be reconciled on an actual view of the spot. For, when approaching it from the east, hillocks of drifted sand, accumulated round the walls, have obtained an elevation almost equal to them, so that the ground within the walls is lower than without. But, towards the sea, the plain closes abruptly in a precipice of some height; so that viewed from that quarter Ascalon may even be said to stand high. The coast runs nearly north-east and south-west. The wall on the seaside rises almost from the water's edge, and is intended to prop the crumbling precipice. It was probably raised on an emergency; for it is composed of rude masonry, where shafts of granite columns are stuck in, so as to represent at a distance the cannon of a ship or the artillery of a fortress. At certain distances on the walls were towers, which, by the parts that still remain, appear to have been of good masonry....

Within the ruins, all was desolation. Fragments of pillars lay scattered about, and elevations here and there showed how many more might lie concealed beneath the surface.

Early on the first of April, Lady Hester, Derwish Mustapha Aga and Mohammed Aga, accompanied by the interpreters and myself, rode over the ruins, seeking for the indications given in the Italian document [disclosing the repositories of immense hoards of money, buried in the city of Ascalon]. The mosque was immediately recognized by the mahreb, or niche, looking towards which the imam stands to direct, as fugelman, the kneeling and prostrations of Mohammedans at prayer. This was still standing, but, in other respects, no more than a stone or two of the foundations remained above ground. Although there was little doubt that this was the spot meant, still it was difficult to know at which side or end, in a building fifty-five paces long and forty-three in breadth, to begin. At the north-west corner of the ruins was a santon's tomb, covered with a small building. Here dwelt a sheikh, the only inhabitant of the place; and, seeing his solitary reign thus molested by horsemen, tents, soldiers and corvées of peasants, he very soon became acquainted with the motive and readily mixed with the spectators. He was consulted as to what he knew of the building. He said that formerly a Barbaresque had visited the shrine and had lived with him eleven months, always lurking about, doing he knew not what: but that, in conversation, he had assigned to two different spots hidden treasures, both within the circuit of the mosque. It was finally resolved to begin on the south side.

The tents were then fixed in the following manner. On the east side, close to the mosque, were planted Signor Catafago's, Mâlem Musa's, M. Beaudin's and my own, each as large as an English marquee: and, close to them, a sewán, or open tent, for meals. The meals were to be served three times a day, consisting of two services at noon and sunset, and of a light breakfast at sunrise. Nowhere in Syria did I fare better than here. At the south side of the mosque, on an eminence or mound, was fixed a large tent of observation, in which Mohammed Aga when present sat. But the tents of Mohammed Aga and the Zaym were without the city walls, close by the eastern gate, in a sandy bottom. And here too were the tents of the cavalry, the kitchens, the water-carriers, the horses, etc.; presenting a scene of showy gaiety almost as lively as a race-course. All the tents were either green or blue: and the principal ones were conspicuous for flaming swords, flowers, stars and other ornaments, worked upon them. Couriers were coming and going every day from Jaffa.

...north of the ruins there was a small village, called El Jura, 200 yards from the walls.

*Ascalon, by David Roberts*

Here two cottages were swept out, matted and carpeted for Lady Hester and her female attendants: for to have encamped in the midst of the men would, by Mohammedans, so far as related to women, have been thought improper, and her ladyship now required the strictest decorum of behaviour in her women, and on all occasions consonant to Mohammedan usages: so that not even Mrs Fry, her English maid, was suffered to open the door of the courtyard without veiling her face. Between the village and the ruins was fixed a tent, and here Lady Hester sat in the daytime and received visits from the agas, the mâlems, etc. At two she generally mounted her ass and rode to see the workmen. On these occasions they would shout and renew their digging with fresh activity....

After digging down three or four feet, some foundations were laid open, running east and west. On removing the earth between them nothing was found but mould and loose stones, with two or three human bones. Three fragments of marble shafts of pillars were bared and a Corinthian capital...

On the third day, the excavations continued along the south wall. The men worked with great animation. The idea of discovering immense heaps of gold seemed to have an effect upon them, although they could not hope for a share in it. On this day there was a great fall of rain and hail, and the weather was so tempestuous as much to impede the labourers. A pipe and tabor were therefore brought, to the tune of which they worked, sung and danced. Cross foundations were met with, running east and west, seeming to have served for the support of rows of pedestals. About fifteen feet from the centre of the south wall were discovered several large fragments of granite columns, which lay one on another in such a manner as to render it probably that they were placed there.

On the fourth day the work was continued nearly in the same direction. At three in the afternoon the workmen struck a mutilated statue. I was immediately called and felt exultation at the sight of a relic of antiquity, which I thought might give celebrity to our labours. The soil around it being removed, it was drawn up by ropes, without damage. There were at the same spot some imperfect remains of the pedestal on which it had stood. The depth of the mould and rubbish which lay over the statue was six or eight feet.

On examination, it proved to be a marble statue of colossal dimensions and of good execution. It was headless and had lost an arm and a leg; but was not otherwise disfigured. It seemed to have represented a deified king: for the shoulders were ornamented with the insignia of the thunderbolt and the breast of Medusa's head. There was every reason to believe that, in the changes of masters which Ascalon had undergone, the place in which we were now digging had originally been a heathen temple, afterwards a church, then a mosque. The statue probably belonged to the age of the successors of Alexander, or it might be that of Herod himself....

On the fifth day the outline of the foundations of the entire building was made out. It was amusing at this time to find how many wise men, some calling themselves astrologers, and some fortune-tellers, started up on all sides to foretell Lady Hester's success. This was fortunate: for the workmen had begun to relax in their labours, and their overseers sneered at the business. Mohammed Aga found his own purposes answered in the number of marble slabs that were discovered. These he shipped, in a coasting-boat, for Jaffa. On the outside of the west foundation, three subterraneous places were opened, which at first, it was thought, would lead to the object we were in search of. But they proved to be cisterns or reservoirs for rain water, with no appearance of antiquity about them; and, both in the round mouth upwards and in the conduit which led the water into them, resembled those in use throughout Syria at the present day....

I had by this time made a pen sketch of the statue and had represented to Lady Hester that her labours, if productive of no golden treasures, had brought to light one more valuable in the eyes of the lovers of the fine arts, and that future travellers would come to visit the ruins of Ascalon, rendered memorable by the enterprise of a woman, who, though digging for gold, yet rescued the remains of antiquity from oblivion. What was my astonishment when she answered – 'This may be true; but it is my intention to break the statue, and have it thrown into the sea, precisely in order that such a report may not get abroad and I lose with the Porte all the merit of my disinterestedness.'

When I heard what her intentions were, I made use of every argument in my power to dissuade her from it; telling her that the apparent vandalism of such an act could never be wiped away in the eyes of virtuosi and would be less excusable, as I was not aware that the Turks had either claimed the statue or had forbidden its preservation. It was true, that, whilst sketching it, the people had expressed their surmises at what I could find to admire in a broken image; and I heard some of them conjecture that it might be a deity of the Frank, as it had been of the Romans and Greeks. But no idle notions, I insisted, ought to have weight on her mind; and I begged hard that, if she could not with decency carry it away, she would at least leave it for others to look at. She replied, 'Malicious people may say I came to search for antiquities for my country and not for treasure for the Porte: so, go this instant; take with you half-a-dozen stout fellows and break it in a thousand pieces!' Her resolution was not a thing of the moment: she had reflected on it two days; and knowing her unalterable determination on such occasions, I went and did as she desired. When Mohammed Aga saw what had been done, he could not conceal his vexation: for it is probable that Lady Hester had read what was passing in his mind and had thus prevented many an insinuation against her. Indeed, reports were afterwards circulated that the chest of the statue was found full of gold – half of which was given to the pasha, and the other half kept by Lady Hester. In England, where her motives were unknown, people have naturally decried her conduct, although it is plain that her strict integrity ought to prove her justification.

On the 9th, when the granite pillars were removed, a work of no trifling magnitude, considering the means by which they were effected, the troughs were found empty. The disappointment was very great; and the more so as the excavation of the four following days produced nothing but two granite columns at the north-west angle, six or eight feet below the surface, a white marble pedestal, some bones of animals and two earthenware lamps … when every research was fruitless, the closing hand was, by Lady Hester's consent, put to our labours on the 14th of April, being a fortnight from the commencement.…Thus ended this most interesting experiment; which failed in its primary object, but had the desirable effect of establishing Lady Hester's popularity throughout Syria and of confirming the belief, already grown up, that she was a person of some consideration, even in the eyes of the Sublime Porte.

# ARTHUR PENHRYN STANLEY

## 1815–81

*Arthur Penhryn Stanley*

*Arthur Penhryn Stanley was born at Alderley Rectory, Cheshire, on 13 December 1815. He was educated at Rugby under Dr Arnold and gained a scholarship to Balliol College, Oxford, in 1833. After a distinguished academic record, having won the Ireland and Newdigate prizes, he was elected a fellow of University College and took orders. In July 1840, Stanley left England for a prolonged tour through Switzerland, Italy, Greece and Sicily. This journey confirmed his love of travel and henceforward scarcely a year passed without his making a voyage abroad. He returned to Oxford in May 1841 and, by 1843, he had been ordained a priest and appointed a college tutor. For the next few years he pursued a literary career, publishing his classic* Life and Correspondence of Dr Arnold *in 1844, alongside his tutorial duties. He also published a series of sermons that he had preached between 1846 and 1847. In July 1851, he accepted a canonry at Canterbury and left Oxford. At the same time he had been appointed secretary of the Oxford University Commission and was instrumental in writing its report, which was issued in 1852. Thereupon he started on a tour of Egypt and the Holy Land, which led to his most popular book,* Sinai and Palestine, *in 1856. That year he was also appointed Professor of Ecclesiastical History at Oxford. In 1862, he was asked to accompany the Prince of Wales on his tour of the East, and the sermons he preached on that tour – as well as some of their experiences – were published in* Sermons in the East *(1863). In 1864, he was installed as Dean of Westminster Abbey and soon made his mark in this new position – although, despite his tolerance, charity and sympathy, High Church Anglicans could never forgive him for championing Colenso and for preaching in Scottish Presbyterian pulpits. His Memorial of Westminster Abbey was published in 1868. Having married late, in 1863, Stanley was said to have never recovered from the death of his wife in 1876. He himself died in 1881 and was buried in Westminster Abbey.*

### The Mosque of Hebron, 1862

There were formerly four sanctuaries in Palestine, which Mussulman jealousy carefully guarded from the approach of Christians. These were the Mosque of Omar and the Mosque of David at Jerusalem, the Great Mosque at Damascus and the Mosque of Hebron. Of these, however, the first and third had within the last few years become accessible, and to these every facility of access was given to the Prince of Wales on the present occasion. The second was of too dubious a character ... to justify any strong demand for its inspection. But the fourth, the Mosque of Hebron, in other words the Sanctuary, first Jewish, then Christian, now Mussulman, which is supposed to cover the Cave of Machpelah – is, of all the Holy Places in Palestine, the one which has excited in modern times the keenest curiosity, and which at the same time rests on the best historical evidence....

While the other sacred places in Palestine ... have been thrown open, at least to distinguished travellers, the Mosque of Hebron still remained, even to royal personages, hermetically sealed.

To break through this mystery, to clear up this uncertainty, even irrespectively of the extraordinary interest attaching to the spot, was felt by those most concerned to be an object not unworthy of the first visit of a Prince of Wales to the Holy Land.

From the moment that the expedition was definitively arranged in January 1862, it was determined by His Royal Highness and his advisers that the attempt should be made, if it were found compatible with prudence, and with the respect due to the religious feelings of the native population. On arriving at Jerusalem, an enquiry immediately arose as to the possibility of accomplishing this long-cherished design. Mr Finn, then the English consul, had already prepared the way, by requesting a firman from the Porte for this purpose. The government at Constantinople, aware of the susceptible fanaticism of the population of Hebron, sent, instead of a direct order, a vizierial letter of recommendation to the Governor of Jerusalem, leaving in fact the whole matter to his discretion. The Governor, Suraya Pasha, partly from the natural difficulties of the proposed attempt, partly, it may be from his own personal feeling on the subject – held out long and strenuously against taking upon himself the responsibility of a step which had hitherto no precedent....The negotiation devolved on General Bruce, the Governor of the Prince of Wales....It may truly be said ... that the tact and firmness which he showed on this occasion were worthy of the first rank of diplomacy....

Suraya Pasha offered every other civility or honour that could be paid. The General took his position on the ground that, since the opening of the other Holy Places, this was the one honour left for the Turkish government to award on the rare occasion of a visit of the Prince of Wales. He urged, too, the feeling with which the request was made: that we, as well as they, had a common interest in the Patriarchs common to both religions; and that nothing was claimed beyond what would be accorded to Mussulmans themselves. At last the Pasha appeared to give way. But a new alarm arose out of a visit of the Royal party to the shrine commonly called the Tomb of David, in Jerusalem [when the Pasha had to send a troop of soldiers to the Prince's rescue from an angry crowd of Mussulmen]....

The difficulties raised in this attempt naturally complicated the question, in which the Prince was chiefly interested, of the access to Hebron; and in the course of that evening the

Pasha finally declared that the responsibility was too grave, and that he could not undertake to guarantee the Prince's safety from the anger, either of the population of Hebron, or of the Patriarchs themselves, who were always on the watch within their tombs to avenge any injury or affront to 'their sanctity'.

It was an anxious moment. On the one hand, there was the doubt, now seriously raised, as to the personal safety of the attempt....On the other hand, the point having been once raised, could not be lightly laid aside.... General Bruce adopted a course which ultimately proved successful. He announced to the Pasha the extreme displeasure of the Prince at the refusal, and declared his intention of leaving Jerusalem instantly for the Dead Sea; adding that, if the sanctuary at Hebron could not be entered, the Prince would decline to visit Hebron altogether. We started immediately on a three days' expedition, the usual excursion to Bethlehem, the Dead Sea and Jericho....

We descended upon the magnificent gorge of the convent of Mar Saba, and in a small platform in the gorge found our own tents pitched. But close by was a smaller encampment, which contained Suraya Pasha – nominally to secure the Prince's safe passage through the disturbed Arab tribes, but really to reopen the negotiations about Hebron. He had followed us by the more direct route from Jerusalem, and on that same evening sent a formal message offering to make the attempt, if the numbers were limited to the Prince and two or three of the suite, and promising to go himself to Hebron to prepare for the event. This proposal was guardedly, but decisively accepted.

Early on the morning of Monday, the 7th of April, we left our encampment and moved in a southerly direction. The object of our journey was mentioned to no one. On our way, we were joined by Dr Rosen, the Prussian consul at Jerusalem, well known to travellers in Palestine, from his profound knowledge of sacred geography, and, in this instance, doubly valuable as a companion, from the special attention which he had paid to the topography of Hebron and its neighbourhood. Before our arrival at Hebron, the Pasha had made every preparation to ensure the safety of the experiment. What he feared was, no doubt, a random shot or stone from some individual fanatic, who might have held his life cheap at the cost of avenging what he thought an outrage on the sanctities of his religion. Against Indian pilgrims, who are well known to hang about these sacred places, we had been especially warned, and one or two such we did in fact meet on our way and on our return. Accordingly, as the protracted file wound through the narrow valley by which the town of Hebron is approached, underneath the walls of those vineyards on the hill-sides, which have made the vale of Eshcol immortal, the whole road on either side for more than a mile was lined with soldiers. The native population, which usually on the Prince's approach to a town streamed out to meet him, was invisible, it may be from compulsion, it may be from silent indignation. We at length reached the green sward in front of the town, crowned by the Quarantine and the Governor's residence. There Suraya Pasha received us. It had been arranged, in accordance with the Pasha's limitation of the numbers, that His Royal Highness should be accompanied, besides the General, by the two members of the party who had given most attention to biblical pursuits, so as to make it evident that the visit was not one of mere curiosity, but had also a distinct scientific purpose. It was, however, finally conceded by the Governor, that the whole of the suite should be included, amounting to seven persons besides the Prince. The servants remained behind. We started on foot, two and two, between two files of soldiers, by the ancient pool of Hebron, up the narrow streets of the modern town, still lined with soldiers. Hardly a face was visible as we passed through; only here and there a solitary guard, stationed at a vacant window, or on the flat roof of a projecting house, evidently to guarantee the safety of the party from any chance missile. It was, in fact, a complete military occupation of th town. At length we reached the south-

*View of Hebron showing the Mosque covering the Cave of Machpelah (photo by Frank Mason Good)*

eastern corner of the massive wall of enclosure, the point at which enquiring travellers from generation to generation have been checked in their approach to this, the most ancient and the most authentic of all the Holy Places of the Holy Land. 'Here', said Dr Rosen, 'was the furthest limit of my researches.' Up the steep flight of the exterior staircase – gazing close at hand on the polished surface of the wall, amply justifying Josephus's account of the marble-like appearance of the huge stones which compose it – we rapidly mounted. At the head of the staircase, which by its long ascent showed that the platform of the Mosque was on the uppermost slope of the hill, and therefore above the level where, if anywhere, the sacred cave would be found, a sharp turn at once brought us within the precincts, and revealed to us for the first time the wall from the inside. A later wall of Mussulman times has been built on the top of the Jewish enclosure. The enclosure itself, as seen from the inside, rises but a few feet above the platform.

Here we were received with much ceremony by five or six persons, corresponding to the dean and canons of a Christian cathedral. They were the representatives of the forty hereditary guardians of the Mosque.

We passed at once through an open court into the Mosque. With regard to the building itself, two points at once became apparent. First, it was clear that it had been originally a Byzantine church. To anyone acquainted with the cathedral of S. Sophia at Constantinople, and with the monastic churches of Mount Athos, this is evident from the double narthex or portico, and from the four pillars of the nave. Secondly, it was clear that it had been converted at a much later period into a mosque. This is indicated by the pointed arches and by the truncation of the apse. The transformation was said by the guardians of the Mosque to have been made by Sultan Kelaoun. The whole building occupies (to speak roughly) one-third of the platform....It will be seen that up to this point no mention has been made of the subject of the greatest interest, namely, the sacred cave itself, in which one at least of the patriarchal family may possibly still repose intact – the embalmed body of Jacob. It may be well supposed that to this object our enquiries were throughout directed. One indication alone of the cavern beneath was visible. In the interior of the Mosque, at the corner of the shrine of Abraham, was a small circular hole, about eight inches across, of which one foot above the pavement was built of strong masonry, but of which the lower part, as far as we could see and feel, was of the living rock. This cavity appeared to open into a dark space beneath, and that space (which the guardians of the Mosque believed to extend under the whole platform) can hardly be anything else than the ancient cavern of Machpelah. This was the only aperture which the guardians recognized. Once, they said, 2,500 years ago, a servant of a great king had penetrated through some other entrance. He descended in full possession of his faculties and of remarkable corpulence; he returned blind, deaf, withered and crippled. Since then the entrance was closed, and this aperture alone was left, partly for the sake of allowing the holy air of the cave to escape into the Mosque and be scented by the faithful; partly for the sake of allowing a lamp to be let down by a chain which we saw suspended at the mouth, to burn upon the sacred grave. We asked whether it could not be lighted now? 'No,' they said; 'the saint likes to have a lamp at night, but not in the full daylight.'

With that glimpse into the dark void we and the world without must for the present be satisfied....

It seems to our notions almost incredible that Christians and Mussulmans, each for a period of 600 years, should have held possession of the sanctuary and not had the curiosity to explore what to us is the one object of interest – the cave. But the fact is undoubted that no account exists of any such attempt....Suraya Pasha himself, a man of considerable intelligence, professed that he had never thought of visiting the Mosque of Hebron for any other purpose than that of snuffing the sacred air, and he had never, till we arrived at Jerusalem, seen the wonderful convent of Mar Saba, or the Dead Sea or the Jordan....

The result of the Prince's visit will have been disappointing to those who expected a more direct solution of the mysteries of Hebron. But it has not been without its indirect benefits. In the first place, by the entrance of the Prince of Wales, the first step has been taken for the removal of the bar of exclusion from this most sacred and interesting spot....And Englishmen may fairly rejoice that this advance in the cause of religious tolerance (if it may so be called) and of biblical knowledge, was attained in the person of the heir to the English throne, out of regard to the position which he and his country hold in the Eastern world.

In the second place, the visit has enabled us to form a clearer judgement of the value of the previous accounts, to correct their deficiencies and to rectify their confusion....To discover the entrance of the cave, to examine the actual places of the patriarchal sepulture, and to set (eyes if so be) on the embalmed body of Jacob, the only patriarch the preservation of whose remains is thus described – must be reserved for the explorers of another generation, for whom this visit will have been the best preparation.

# JOHN LLOYD STEPHENS

## 1805–52

*John Lloyd Stephens was born in New Jersey, USA, in 1805. He graduated from Columbia College in 1822 and then read law. At the age of twenty he gratified his insatiable wanderlust by journeying to Arkansas. Bored by the law, he left America in 1834 and spent two years seeking the unusual in the Mediterranean, the Holy Land and Eastern Europe. With the publication of his two books on these travels –* Incidents of Travel in Egypt, Arabia Petraea and the Holy Land *(1837) and* Incidents of Travel in Greece, Turkey, Russia and Poland *(1838), he soon became famous as the 'American traveller'. A democrat, he was sent in 1839 on a confidential diplomatic mission to Central America, where he also investigated the ruins of Honduras, Guatemala and the Yucatan. His* Incidents of Travel in Central America *appeared in 1841. That year he also returned to Central America for a more extensive study. He next became a promoter of the Ocean Steam Navigation Company and started a line in 1847; he was also an active supporter of the Hudson River Railroad. The last great work he was involved in was the establishment of the Panama Railroad. He spent two winters there personally supervising the work, but caught a disease in Panama and died on his return to New York in 1852.*

### A Patriarchal Feast

I have before mentioned that among these barren and desolate mountains, there was frequently a small space of ground, near some fountain or deposit of water, known only to the Arabs, capable of producing a scanty crop of grass to pasture a few camels and a small flock of sheep or goats. There the Bedouin pitches his tent and remains till the scant produce is consumed; and then packs up his household goods and seeks another pasture ground....In fact, the life of the Bedouin, his appearance and habits, are precisely the same as those of the patriarchs of old. Abraham himself, the first of the patriarchs, was a Bedouin, and 4,000 years have not made the slightest alteration in the character or habits of this extraordinary people....

The woman whom we had pursued belonged to the tent of a Bedouin not far from our road, but completely hidden from our view; and, when overtaken by Toualeb [the guide], she recognized in him a friend of her tribe, and in the same spirit, and almost in the same words which would have been used by her ancestors, 4,000 years ago, she asked us to her tent and promised us a lamb or a kid for supper. Her husband was stretched on the ground in front of his tent and welcomed us with an air and manner that belonged to the desert, but which a king on his throne could not have excelled. He was the embodied personification of all my conceptions of a patriarch. A large loose frock, a striped handkerchief on his head, bare legs, sandals on his feet and a long white beard, formed the outward man. Almost immediately after we were seated, he took his shepherd's crook, and, assisted by his son, selected a lamb from the flock, for the evening meal. And now I would fain prolong the illusion of this pastoral scene: to stop at the door of an Arab's tent, and partake with him of a lamb or kid prepared by his hospitable hands, all sitting together on the ground, and provided with no other implements than those which nature gave us, is a picture of primitive and captivating simplicity; but the details were such as to destroy for ever all its poetry, and take away all relish for patriarchal feasts. While we were taking coffee, the lamb lay bleating in our ears, as if conscious of its coming fate; and this was not particularly gratifying. The coffee drunk and the pipe smoked, our host arose and laid his hand upon the victim: the long sword, which he wore over his shoulder, was quickly drawn: one man held the head and another the hind legs; and, with a rapidity almost inconceivable, it was killed and dressed, and its smoking entrails, yet curling with life, were broiling on the fire.

I was the guest of the evening, and had no reason to complain of the civility of my entertainer; for, with the air of a well-bred host, and an epicure to boot, he drew from the burning coals one of the daintiest pieces, about a yard and a half in length, and, rolling one end between the palms of his hands to a tapering point, broke off about a foot and handed it to me. Now I was by no means dainty. I could live upon the coarsest fare, and all the little luxuries of tables, knives and forks were of very little moment in my estimation. I was prepared to go the full length in this patriarchal feast. But my indifference was not proof against the convivial elegancies of my Bedouin companions; and, as I saw yard after yard disappear, like long strings of macaroni, down their capacious throats, I was cured of all poetical associations and my appetite together.

In the tent of the Arabian patriarch, woman, the pride, the ornament and the charm of domestic life, is the mere household drudge. In vain may one listen for her light footstep, or look to find her by the side of her natural lord, giving a richer charm to the hospitality he is extending to a stranger. It would repay one for much of the toil and monotony of a journey in the desert, if, when by chance he found himself at a Bedouin tent, he would be greeted by her sunny smile....But this the customs of the tribes forbid. When the stranger approaches, the woman retires....Nor is this the worst of her lot. Even when alone, the wife of the Bedouin is not regarded as his equal: the holy companionship of wedded life has, between them, no existence....Away, then, with all dreams of superior happiness in this more primitive condition of society! Captivating as is the wild idea of roving abroad at will, unfettered by the restraints of law, or of conventional observances, the meanest tenant of a log-hut in our western prairies has sources of happiness which the wandering Arab can never know.

One word as to the hospitality of the Arabs. I had read beautiful descriptions of its manifestation, and in some way or other had gathered up the notion that the Bedouin would be offended by an offer to reward his hospitality with a price; but, feeling naturally anxious not to make a blunder on either side of a question so delicate, I applied to my guide, Toualeb, for information on the subject. His answer was brief and explicit. He said there was no obligation to give or pay, it being the custom of the Bedouin (among friendly tribes) to ask the wayfaring man into his tent, give him food and shelter, and send him on his way in the morning; that I could give or not, as I pleased; but that, if I did not, the hospitable host would wish his lamb alive again: and, from the exceeding satisfaction with which that estimable person received my parting gift, I am very sure that, in this instance at least, I did better in taking Toualeb's knowledge of his people for my guide than I should have done by acting upon what I had read in books. It may be that, if I had gone among them poor and friendless, I should have been received in the same manner, and nothing would have been expected or received from me; but I am inclined to think, from what I saw afterwards, that in such case, the lamb would have been spared for a longer term of existence, and the hospitality confined to a dip into the dish and a mat at the door of the tent....

*Bargaining with the Bedouin, Hebron, 1836*

As we approached Hebron, the sheikh became more civil and obsequious and, before we came in sight of the city, he seemed to have some misgivings about entering it and asked me

A Bedouin sheikh

to secure protection from the governor for that night for himself and men, which I did not hesitate to promise. I was glad to be approaching again a place under the established government of the pasha, where, I was sure of protection against the exactions of my Bedouins; and the reader may judge of the different degrees of security existing in these regions from being told that I looked to the protection of a Turk as a guarantee against the rapacity of an Arab....

As soon as we came in sight of the city, the sheikh dismounted and made Paul [a travelling companion] take back his dromedary and gave me my horse, and drawing up the caravan with the order and precision of a troop of 'regulars', we made a dashing entry ... leaving the baggage camels at the gate, with our horses and dromedaries at full gallop, we dashed through the streets to the door of the citadel and demanded an audience of the governor. The Turks and Arabs are proverbial for the indifference with which they look upon everything; and, though I knew that a stranger coming from the desert was a rare object and ought to excite some attention, I was amused and surprised at the extraordinary sensation our appearance created. Men stopped in the midst of their business; the lazy groups in the cafes sprang up, and workmen threw down their tools to run out and stare at us. I was surprised at this; but I afterwards learned that since the pasha had disarmed all Syria, and his subjects in that part of his dominions wore arms only by stealth, it was a startling occurrence to see a party of Bedouins coming in from the desert, armed to the very teeth and riding boldly up to the gates of the citadel....

...I expected a scene with them at parting and I was not disappointed.... I counted out the price of the camels and laid down a bakshish for each. Not one of them touched it, but all looked at the money and at me alternately, without speaking a word (it was about ten times as much as I would have had to pay for the same services anywhere else); and the sheikh seemed uncertain what to do. The janissary, whose presence I had almost forgotten, put himself forward as an actor in the scene, and half drawing his sword, swore that it was a vile extortion; that the governor ought to know of it; and that the firman of the pasha ought to protect a stranger. This brought the sheikh to a decision; and, taking up his own portion, and directing them to do the same, he expressed himself satisfied, and betook himself to smoking. It was evident that he was not altogether content; and, the janissary leaving us soon after, all turned upon me and gave voice to their dissatisfaction.... I am well satisfied that if the denouement had taken place in the desert, they would have searched for themselves whether there was not something left in the bottom of my trunk; and, from what happened afterwards, I am very sure that they would have stripped me of my Turkish plumage; but now I was perfectly safe....I told them I cared not whether they were satisfied or not. As I rose, the sheikh fell; and when I began working myself into a passion at his exorbitant demand, he fell to begging a dollar or two in such moving terms that I could not resist. I continued yielding to his extortions, until, having ascertained the expense, I found that I had not a dollar more than enough to carry me to Jerusalem; and at this moment he consummated his impudence by begging my dress off my back. The dress was of no great value; it had not cost much when new, and was travel-worn and frayed with hard usage; but it had a value in my eyes from the circumstance of having been worn upon this journey. I had given him nearly all my tent equipage, arms, ammunition, etc., and I had borne with all his extortions; but he urged and insisted, and begged and entreated with so much pertinacity, that my patience was exhausted, and I told him that I had borne with him long enough and that he and his whole tribe might go to the d---l....Now the long smothered passion broke out and, clamorous as the Arabs always were, I had never seen them so furious. They raved like so many bedlamites; and the sheikh drew from his bosom his portion, dashed it on the floor, swearing that no Frank should ever pass through his country again, poured out upon me a volley of curses and, grinding his teeth with disappointment, rushed out of the room....

A moment after he had gone, I was sorry for what had happened, particularly on account of his oath that no European should ever pass through his country. I felt unhappy in the idea that, when I expected to be the pioneer in opening a new and interesting route, I had become the means of more effectually closing it. With a heavy heart I told Paul that I must have another interview; that the old dress must go and anything else I had; and that I must have peace upon any terms. To dispose of this business, in about an hour the sheikh returned with his brother and, kissing my hand, told me that he had just heard of a robbery on the road to Jerusalem, and came to tell me of it; and added that he felt unhappy at having left me in anger; that he had been so used to sitting with me that he could not remain away.

I was not to be outdone; and I introduced him to my Jewish companions as my dearest friend, the chief of the tribe of El Alouins, who had protected me with his life through the dangers of the desert, and to whose arm they were indebted for the privilege of seeing my face. The sheikh looked at me as if he thought me in earnest, and himself entitled to all that I had said....

This over, we bade each other farewell, the sheikh and his swarthy companions kissing me on both sides of my face. I looked after them as long as they continued in sight, listened till I heard the last clattering of their armour, and I never saw, nor do I ever wish to see them, again.

One by one I had seen my waking dreams fade away; the pictures of oriental scenes melt into nothing; but I had still clung to the simplicity and purity of the children of the desert, their temperance, their contented poverty and contempt for luxuries, as approaching the true nobility of man's nature, and sustaining the poetry of the 'land of the East'. But my last dream was broken; and I never saw, among the wanderers of the desert, any traits of character, or habits of life, which did not make me value more the privileges of civilization....

# WILLIAM MAKEPEACE THACKERAY

### ◄━ 1811–63 ━►

*William Makepeace Thackeray, c.1840 (portrait by D. Machise)*

*William Makepeace Thackeray was born in Calcutta in 1811. When he was six he was sent back to England to be educated, but later left Cambridge without a degree due to gambling debts. He began his writing career by becoming the proprietor of the* National Standard, *which ceased publication after a year, and then lived in Paris, contributing regularly to a number of publications. In 1842 he began his famous association with* Punch. The Snobs of England *appeared there in 1846–7 and* Mr Punch's Prize Novelists *in 1847. However, it was not until 1847 that his first major novel,* Vanity Fair, *was published.* Pendennis *followed in 1848. In July 1844, Thackeray undertook 'an excursion' along the shores of the Mediterranean, which he chronicled in his amusing* From Cornhill to Grand Cairo *(1846). As well as writing major novels, he continued to contribute to* Punch *until 1854 and twice visited America in the 1850s on a highly successful lecture tour.* The Virginians, *partly set there, began to appear on his return in 1857. In 1860 he became the first editor of the Cornhill Magazine, where much of his later work was published.*

*Landing at Jaffa*

On the 3rd October our cable rushed with a huge rattle into the blue sea before Jaffa, at a distance of considerably more than a mile of the town, which lay before us very clear, with the flags of the consuls flaring in the bright sky, and making a cheerful hospitable show. The houses a great heap of sun-baked stones, surmounted here and there by minarets and countless little white-washed domes; a few date trees spread out their fan-like heads over these dull-looking buildings; long sands stretched away on either side, with low purple hills behind them; we could see specks of camels crawling over these yellow plains; and those persons who were about to land had the leisure to behold the sea-spray flashing over the sands and over a heap of black rocks which lie before the entry to the town.

When the danger of the rocks and surf was passed, came another danger of the hideous brutes in brown skins and the briefest shirts, who came towards the boat, straddling through the water with outstretched arms, grinning and yelling their Arab invitations to mount their shoulders. I think these fellows frightened the ladies still more than the rocks and the surf; but the poor creatures were obliged to submit, and trembling were accommodated somehow upon the mahogany backs of these ruffians, carried through the shallows and flung up to a ledge before the city gate, where crowds more of dark people were swarming, howling after their fashion. The gentlemen, meanwhile, were having arguments about the eternal bakshish with the roaring Arab boatmen....

Being cast upon the ledge, the first care of our gallantry was to look after the ladies, who were scared and astonished by the naked savage brutes, who were shouldering them to and fro; and bearing them through these and a dark archway, we came into a street crammed with donkeys and their packs and drivers, and towering camels with leering eyes looking into the second-floor rooms, and huge splay feet, through which mesdames and mesdemoiselles were to be conducted. We made a rush at the first open door and passed comfortably under the heels of some horses gathered under the arched court and up a stone staircase, which turned out to be that of the Russian consul's house. His people welcomed us most cordially to his abode, and the ladies and the luggage (objects of our solicitude) were led up many stairs and across several terraces to a most comfortable little room, under a dome of its own, where the representative of Russia sat. Women with brown faces and draggle-tailed coats and turbans, and wondering eyes, and no stays, and blue beads and gold coins hanging round their necks, came to gaze as they passed upon the fair neat English women; blowsy black cooks puffing over fires, and the strangest pots and pans on the terraces; children paddling about in long striped robes, interrupted their sports or labours, to come and stare; and the consul, in his cool domed chamber, with a lattice overlooking the sea, with clean mats and pictures of the Emperor, the Virgin and St George, received the strangers with smiling courtesies, regaling these with pomegranates and sugar, those with pipes of tobacco, whereof the fragrant tubes were three yards long.

The Russian amenities concluded, we left the ladies still under the comfortable, cool dome of the Russian consulate and went to see our own representative. The streets of the little town are neither agreeable to horse or foot travellers. Many of the streets are mere flights of rough steps, leading abruptly into private houses; you pass under archways and passages numberless; a steep, dirty labyrinth of stone-vaulted stables and sheds occupy the ground floor of the habitations; and you pass from flat to flat of the terraces; at various irregular corners of which little chambers, with little private domes, are erected; and the people live seemingly as much upon the terrace as in the room.

We found the English consul in a queer little arched chamber, with a strange picture of the King's arms to decorate one side of it; and here the consul, a demure old man, dressed in red flowing robes, with a feeble janissary, bearing a shabby tin-mounted staff, or mace, to denote his office, received such of our nation as came to him for hospitality. He distributed pipes and coffee to all and everyone; he made us a present of his house and all his beds for the night, and went himself to lie quietly on the terrace; and for all this hospitality he declined to receive any reward from us and said he was but doing his duty in taking us in. This worthy man, I thought, must doubtless be very well paid by our government for making such sacrifices; but it appears that he does not get one single farthing, and that the greater number of our Levant consuls are paid at a similar rate of easy remuneration. If we have bad consular agents, have we a right to complain?

The active young men of our party had been on shore long before us and seized upon all the available horses in the town; but we relied upon a letter from Halil Pasha, enjoining all governors and pashas to help us in all ways; and hearing we were the bearers of this document, the cadi and vice-governor of Jaffa came to wait upon the head of our party, declared that it was his delight to do everything in the world to serve us; that there were no horses, unluckily, but he would send and get some in three hours; and so left us with a world of grinning bows and many choice compliments, from one side to the other, which came to each filtered through an obsequious interpreter. But hours passed, and the clatter of horses hoofs was not heard. We had our dinner of eggs and flaps of bread, and the sunset gun fired: we had our pipes and coffee again, and the night fell…. We determined to go and seek in his own den this shuffling dispenser of infidel justice….The poor consul got a lamp for us with a bit of wax candle, such as I wonder his means could afford; the shabby janissary marched ahead with his tin mace, the two laquais de place, that two of our company had hired, stepped forward, each with an old sabre, and we went clattering and stumbling down the streets of the town, in order to seize upon this cadi in his own divan….

As piety forbids the Turks to eat during the weary daylight hours of Ramadan, they spend their time profitably sleeping until the welcome sunset, when the town wakens: all the lanterns are lighted up; all the pipes begin to puff, and the narghiles to bubble; all the sour-milk-and-sherbert-men begin to yell out the excellence of their wares; all the frying pans in the little, dirty cook-shops begin to frizz, and the pots to send forth a steam: and through this dingy, ragged, bustling, beggarly cheerful scene, we began now to march towards the Bow Street of Jaffa. We bustled through a crowded narrow archway which led to the cadi's police-office, entered the little room, atrociously perfumed with musk, and passing by the rail-board, where the common sort stood, mounted up the stage on which his worship and friends sat, and squatted down on the divans in stern and silent dignity. His honour ordered us coffee, his countenance evidently showing considerable alarm. A black slave, whose duty seemed to be to prepare this beverage in a side-room with a furnace, prepared for each of us about a tea-spoonful of the liquor: his worship's clerk, I presume, a tall Turk of noble aspect, presented it to us, and having lapped up the little modicum of drink, the British lion began to speak.

All the other travellers (said the lion with perfect reason) have good horses and are gone … but we vizirs in our own country, and coming with letters of Halil Pasha are laughed at, spit upon! Are Halil Pasha's letters dirt, that you attend to them in this way?…and so on. This speech with many variations was made on our side for a quarter of an hour; and we finally swore, that unless the horses were forthcoming, we would write to Halil Pasha the next morning, and to his Excellency the English minister at the Sublime Porte. Then you should have heard the chorus of Turks in reply: a dozen voices rose up from the divan, shouting, screaming, ejaculating, expectorating (the Arab language seems to require a great employment of the two latter oratorical methods), and uttering what the meek

*Jaffa looking south, by David Roberts*

interpreter did not translate to us, but what I dare say were by no means complimentary phrases towards us and our nation. Finally the palaver concluded by the cadi declaring that by the will of heaven horses should be forthcoming at three o'clock in the morning....

We then marched through the bazaars, that were lofty and grim, and pretty full of people. In a desolate broken building, some hundreds of children were playing and singing; in many corners sat parties over their water-pipes, one of whom every now and then would begin twanging out a most queer chant; others there were playing at casino – a crowd squatted round the squalling gamblers, and talking and looking on with eager interest. In one place of the bazaar we found 100 people at least listening to a story-teller, who delivered his tale with excellent action, voice and volubility; in another they were playing a sort of thimble-rig with coffee cups all intent upon the game, and the player himself very wild lest one of our party, who had discovered where the pea lay, should tell the company. The devotion and energy with which all these pastimes were pursued struck me as much as anything. These people have been playing thimble-rig and casino; that story-teller has been shouting his tale of Antar, for forty years; and they are just as happy with this amusement now as when they first tried it. Is there no ennui in the Eastern countries...?

From the bazaars we went to see the house of Mustapha, said to be the best house and the greatest man in Jaffa. But the great man had absconded suddenly and had fled to Egypt. The sultan had made a demand upon him for 16,000 purses, £80,000 – Mustapha retired – the sultan pounced down upon his house and his goods, his horses, his mules. His harem was desolate. We passed from hall to hall, terrace to terrace – a few fellows were slumbering on the naked floors and scarce turned as we went by them. We entered Mustapha's particular divan – there was the raised floor, but no bearded friends squatting away the night of Ramadan; there was the little coffee furnace, but where the slave and the coffee and the glowing embers of the pipes? Mustapha's favourite passages from the Koran were still painted up on the walls, but nobody was the wiser for them....If it be but to read the Arabian Nights again on getting home, it is good to have made this little voyage and seen these strange places and faces.

Then we went out through the arched lowering gateway of the town into the plain beyond, and that was another famous and brilliant scene of Arabian Nights. The heaven shone with a marvellous brilliancy – the plain disappeared far in the haze – the towers and battlements of the town rose black against the sky – old outlandish trees rose up here and there – clumps of camels were couched in the rare herbage – dogs were baying about – groups of men lay sleeping under their haicks round about – round about the tall gates many lights were twinkling – and they brought us water-pipes and sherbet – and we wondered to think that London was only three weeks off.

Then came the night at the consuls. The poor demure old gentleman brought out his mattresses; and the ladies sleeping round on the divans, we lay down quite happy; and I for my part intended to make as delightful dreams as Alnaschar; but – lo, the delicate mosquito sounded his horn: the active flea jumped up and came to feast on Christian flesh (the Eastern flea bites more bitterly than the most savage bug in Christendom) and the bug – oh, the accursed! ... I heard all the cocks in Jaffa crow; the children crying, and the mothers hushing them; the donkeys braying fitfully in the moonlight; at last, I heard the clatter of hoofs below, and the hailing of men. It was three o'clock, the horses were actually come....

# HENRY BAKER TRISTRAM

### 1822–1906

Henry Baker Tristram

Henry Baker Tristram was born in Northumberland in 1822. In 1839 he went to Lincoln College, Oxford, and graduated with a BA in Classics in 1844, proceeding to an MA in 1846. Having been ordained as a deacon in 1845 and a priest in 1846, he became curate of Marchand Bishop, but had to go abroad because of lung trouble. He went to Bermuda, where he became secretary to the governor, Sir William Henry Elliott, and also acted as a naval and military chaplain. It was whilst he was there that he took up the study of birds and shells. In 1849 he became rector of Castle Eden, Co. Durham, but ill-health again drove him abroad to Algeria during the winters of 1855–6 and 1856–7 – he penetrated far into the desert and gathered material for his first book, The Great Sahara (1860). The following winter he visited Palestine and Egypt. Revisiting Palestine in 1863–4, he produced the first of his books on the Holy Land, The Land of Israel: A Journey of Travels in Palestine (1865). He went back to Palestine again in 1880–81, 1894 and 1897, as well as travelling to Japan, China and North-West America. His chief interest lay in the work of the Church Missionary Society and, for forty years, he acted as its representative in the county of Durham. He was also a freemason and, in 1884, was appointed the Grand Chaplain of England; in 1885 he became deputy Grand Master for Durham. His knowledge of the geography, topography and natural history of Palestine was unrivalled and he wrote a number of books on the area, including The Natural History of the Bible (1867), The Topography of the Holy Land (1872), The Land of Moab (1873) and The Flora and Fauna of Palestine (1884). Tristram died in Durham in March 1906.

*From Eingeddi to Masada*

We had our last plunge in the cool water of Wady Sudeir at sunrise; by seven a.m. the tents were struck; and by eight o'clock our long caravan of forty-three beasts had started for Sebbeh. We had an easy day's journey along the shore [of the Dead Sea], only occasionally interrupted by the deep gullies of the dry watercourses through the gravel and boulder deposit, which caused detours and delays, but nothing worse. We were now on the high road used, not for commerce, but by marauding parties from the south and east, since the time when Chedorlaomer and his confederates marched against El Paran. It was a dreary, desolate, hungry ride, more truly reaching the popular notions of the Dead Sea than anything we had yet met with. All around us was utterly lifeless and brown, with the cliffs and mountains glaring red in the sunshine and the soft alluviam below dazzling our eyes by its whiteness....

At half-past one p.m. we reached the foot of Sebbeh (Masada) and halted. Our guides had fully reckoned on finding a supply of water in the Wady Seyâl, the last but one before reaching Sebbeh, but the pools and wells were alike dry. Our whole store consisted of two goatskins full, brought from Ain Jidy. This was a blow to all our plans, for we had intended to spend two days at Sebbeh for exploration, and there were many questions of interest to be solved in the neighbourhood. But with our caravan we must move at once to water. We may have felt angry with our Arabs, who ought to know, but had been too lazy to ascertain, the state of the wells beforehand, but wrath would have been an useless expenditure of energy; there was no time to be lost. B. promptly got out his photographic apparatus, which was shouldered by an Arab, and at once we commenced the ascent to the fortress of Masada. Some of our Bedouin had already been despatched up the adjacent Wady Nemriyeh with goatskins to search for rain pools, and very determinedly we told the thirsty party that we must remain here, water or no water, until next morning.

The difficulty of the ascent to the fortress has been much exaggerated by some writers. An English lady could accomplish it easily, and there is nothing perilous or trying beyond what is of daily occurrence in the rocky mountain paths of the country. Excepting in three places, any person might walk up with his hands in his pockets. We left the camp and mounted on the north side of the ravine, which isolates the citadel to the south of it; and then, getting on to the west side of the mountain across a narrow ravine, clambered by an easy zigzag to the top, while our attendant toiled after us with the camera on his back. In this we were assisted by an enormous causeway, or rather embankment, thrown up by Flavius Silva in the celebrated siege. The whole ascent occupied forty-eight minutes of very hard walking. Once on the top we were richly repaid by a view, the most grand in its sternness and desolate magnificence I ever beheld. A solitary imperial eagle was soaring close above us, and a Lanner falcon was pursuing a small flock of rock pigeons, while a few rock martins (*Cotyle palustris*, Rüpp.), darted past us and swept round the corner of the cliff. These were the only signs of life on this mountain of rocks, sharp, angular and bare, without a green blade or leaf from its foot to its crest, except a few stunted salsolas. Yet even among them I found, in great numbers, a new species of snail (*Helix masadae*, Tristr.), something like a dwarfed and stunted *H. caesariensis*, but with a deeply striated shell, hidden under the stones and in the fissures.

We measured the height of the peak barometrically and found it exactly 2,200 feet above the level of the Dead Sea. This is very much higher than the usual computation, which gives it as from 1,200 to 1,500 feet. But as we found our observations of the height of the bottom of the cliff from the sea-level (554 feet) almost to coincide with those of

Poole (563 feet), I feel disposed to confide in the accuracy of our observations....

When we had reached the top of the causeway, we had a little hard climbing to the edge of the crest and over some half-ruined walls, when we found ourselves in Masada. It is a flat platform, on the summit of a peak, isolated by tremendous chasms on all sides, of an oblong shape, widest at the southern extremity. At the north end it tapers to a promontory, only thirty-two yards wide. Here was placed the strongest part of the fortification. About seventy feet below (so far as we could judge), on a slight projecting ledge, was built a strong circular fort, with double walls, and a hollow space of four feet between them. These walls were perfect; but we found it impossible, without ropes, to descend them, though we got down to within twenty feet and saw several windows, or loopholes, in the solid rock, which we could not reach, but which told us plainly of vast subterranean vaults yet remaining to be explored. A lanner falcon was quietly perched at the point, and on this were the ruins of another fort, quadrangular, and which had once reached up, as we could see by the fragments of masonry, to the base of the round bastion above. Below this the precipice was sheer for 1,000 feet....

As I sat astride a projecting rock on the north peak, I could look down from my giddy height, 1,500 feet, on both sides and in front; and yet so clear was the atmosphere, and so extraordinary its power of conveying sound, that I could carry on a conversation with my friends in the camp below, and compare barometers and observations....

Looking down from the top, the whole of the Dead Sea was spread out as a map, with the low-lying Lisan, Kerak, Mezraah and the Ghor es Safieh distinct in the distance. It was a picture of stern grandeur and desolate magnificence, perhaps unequalled in the world....

## Ain Feshkhah on the Dead Sea

No traveller had yet made an accurate survey of the coast from Ain Feshkhah to Ain Jidy; and upon completing this we had set our hearts. There is something indescribably exciting and interesting in working through a new country, be it ever so small a fragment of unknown ground. Every phenomenon, the most trifling, is noted; every incident is remembered; and if the notes on these should be found dull or prolix, I can only beg that allowance may be made for the importance with which, at the moment, every particular was invested in our eyes.

We enquired of the sheikh whether we could not pass by the Ras (headland), and thence up the gorge to Marsaba. He replied that it was quite impossible and that no one had ever been by that route. I told him that the English for 'impossible' was 'we will try', and set off with my barometer, prismatic compass and gun to see what it was, determined to round the headland and map five miles of coast for my day's work. The sheikh's brother, Jemil, followed me, in duty bound, as my bodyguard. The cane brake soon tapered off to a fine narrow edging, running for a mile along the shore. Then we scrambled among huge boulders, rolled down on to the narrowing beach from the hills above. Here we found a large vein of the bituminous stone or shale, 'stink-stone', from which many of the ornaments sold to pilgrims at Jerusalem are manufactured. The substance seemed to have been partially ejected in a liquid form and to have streamed down the cliffs. It was generally mixed with flints and pebbles, sometimes covering the boulders in large splashes, and then, in the sea itself, formed the matrix of a very hard conglomerate of gravel and flints. When thrown into the fire, it burnt with a sulphurous smell, but would not ignite at the flame of a lamp.

After scrambling on for more than a mile, we found our passage barred, and I took to the water. For some distance there was no difficulty in wading, the sea not reaching to the hips;

*The Dead Sea*

but Jemil, with true national dislike of the element, followed me no further. On coming to the point of the headland, I found the rocks went clear down, from a dizzy height, to an unknown depth, and I had to give up my aquatic excursion. But there was a way of scrambling up the cliff, which I accomplished, sadly incommoded by my gun on my back; and crossing close over the water-line, I scrambled up and down three narrow gullies – the two first, Wady Samâarah and Wady Sakâtah, not being named in the maps, and the third being the main gorge of the Wady en Nâr, or the Kedron, running down from Marsaba. The first of these is flanked on the north side by a trap dyke, which runs boldly out and which appears to account for the projection of the headland. Over the third, the hard crystalline limestone cliffs stand perpendicular, cleft and cracked, looking at first sight like columnar basalt. On crossing it and getting to the other side, I was astonished to find the cliff standing sheer out, not more than fifty yards thick, and a precipice down to a wide plain on the south side. It is strange that the stream should have cut for itself this deep gorge through the very edge of the rock, which forms merely a thin wall on the south, and that it should never have burst through it to the plain. I never saw so thin a wall of rock of so grand a height.

From the top, the view was magnificent. A wide plain, pushing out in several gracefully sweeping sandspits into the sea, was spread at my feet, and did not, at this distance, reveal its barrenness. A strange, conical hill, like a colossal cairn, stood about three miles off isolated, nearly in the centre of the plain, and the view of the low coastline was uninterrupted towards the south, for ten miles, till it reached Ras Mersed, not far from Eingeddi. No map, excepting Lynch's, whose accuracy I have since tested, gives the slightest indications of the indentations and irregularities of the coastline in this quarter, where the contour is more embayed than in any other part of the sea. The plain, though terminating in sandspits, is by no means barren; tamarisk, acacia and retem bushes stud its surface; and the camels of the Ta'âmireh were browsing on its herbage.

I had mounted, so far as I could judge by my barometer (but I rather mistrust the observation, as unfortunately I had not noted the instrument accurately), 1,500 feet above the Dead Sea, and the general range of the mountains of the wilderness of Judea could be distinctly traced running due north and south. Exactly parallel to them, one could follow the line of the eastern mountains from Jebel Ajlun to Kerak, for I had now mounted above the sirocco haze, which obscured everything below with a sandy mist. After wandering some way on the south plain, and taking the bearings at the edge of the spit for the coastline, it was time to return, unless I wished to try the somewhat doubtful hospitality of the Ta'âmireh, who could not be far from their camels. When I should have got back I know not, had I not lighted on an Arab track a little further west, near the crest, which I followed as rapidly as I could, that I might cross the ravines before nightfall. I was overcome with thirst, when I found a little muddy rain-water in a hollow in a rock, which I drank, thankful for the providential provision as Hagar must have been for the well in the wilderness. About a mile from camp I met an Arab sent in quest of me with a bag of water, who told me that L. and several others were searching for me on a path lower down, as they had become alarmed at my absence. It was now dark, and I sent him on to recall the friendly scouts, while I returned thoroughly exhausted, but with the ample reward of having accomplished a very satisfactory piece of surveying.

# MARK TWAIN

### ◀━ 1835–1910 ━▶

Mark Twain

Mark Twain, the pseudonym of Samuel Langhorne Clemens, was born in Florida, Missouri, in 1835. After his father's death in 1847, he was apprenticed to a printer and wrote for his brother's newspaper; from 1857 to 1861 he was a pilot on the Mississippi and from 1862 worked as a newspaper correspondent for various Nevada and Californian magazines, adopting the pseudonym 'Mark Twain' – from a well-known call of the man sounding the river in shallow places ('mark twain' meaning 'by the mark of two fathoms'). Under this name he published his first successful story, 'Jim Smiley and his Jumping Frog', in 1865. This became the title story of The Celebrated Jumping Frog of Calaveras County, and Other Sketches (1867), which established him as a leading humorist. This reputation was consolidated by his book, The Innocents Abroad (1869), the account of a voyage through the Mediterranean and the Holy Land. He later moved to Connecticut and joined a publishing firm which failed, but he largely recouped his losses by writing and lecturing. His two masterpieces, The Adventures of Tom Sawyer (1876) and The Adventures of Huckleberry Finn (1885), which paint an unforgettable picture of Mississippi frontier life, are firmly established among the world's classics. Other favourites are Tramp Abroad (1880) and A Connecticut Yankee in King Arthur's Court (1889), as well as his autobiographical work, Life on the Mississippi (1883). The last two decades of his life were full of financial worries and Twain spent much time and money on trying to recoup funds by writing, undertaking lecture tours and getting involved in various business enterprises.

*Impressions of Nazareth*

At Nazareth we camped in an olive grove near the Virgin Mary's fountain and that wonderful Arab 'guard' came to collect some bakshish for his 'services' in following us from Tiberius and warding off invisible dangers with the terrors of his armament. The dragoman had paid his master, but that counted as nothing – if you hire a man to sneeze for you, here, and another chooses to help him, you have got to pay both. They do nothing whatever without pay. How it must have surprised these people to hear the way of salvation offered to them 'without money and without price'. If the manners, time, the figures and metaphors of the Bible are not the evidence to prove it by.

We entered the great Latin Convent which is built over the traditional dwelling-place of the Holy Family. We went down a flight of fifteen steps below the ground level and stood in a small chapel tricked out with tapestry hangings, silver lamps and oil paintings. A spot marked by a cross, in the marble floor under the altar, was exhibited as the place made for ever holy by the feet of the Virgin when she stood up to receive the message of the angel. So simple, so unpretending a locality to be the scene of so mighty an event! The very scene of the Annunciation – an event which has been commemorated by splendid shrines and august temples all over the civilized world, and one which the princes of art have made it their loftiest ambition to picture worthily on their canvas; a spot whose history is familiar to the very children of every house, and city and obscure hamlet of the furthest lands of Christendom; a spot which myriads of men would toil across the breadth of a world to see, would consider it a priceless privilege to look upon. It was easy to think these thoughts; but it was not easy to bring myself up to the magnitude of the situation. I could sit off several thousand miles and imagine the angel appearing with shadowy wings and lustrous countenance, and note the glory that streamed downward upon the Virgin's head while the message from the Throne of God fell upon her ears – anyone can do that beyond the ocean, but few can do it here. I saw the little recess from which the angel stepped, but could not fill its void. The angels that I know are creatures of unstable fancy – they will not fit into niches of substantial stone. Imagination labours best in distant fields. I doubt if any man can stand in the Grotto of the Annunciation and people with the phantom images of his mind its too tangible walls of stone....

These gifted Latin monks never do anything by halves. If they were to show you the Brazen Serpent that was elevated in the wilderness, you could depend upon it that they had on hand the pole it was elevated on also, and even the hole it stood in. They have got the 'Grotto' of the Annunciation here; and just as convenient to it as one's throat is to his mouth, they have also the Virgin's kitchen, and even her sitting-room, where she and Joseph watched the Infant Saviour play with Hebrew toys 1,800 years ago. All under one roof and all clean, spacious, comfortable 'grottoes'. It seems curious that personages intimately connected with the Holy Family always lived in grottoes – in Nazareth, Bethlehem, in imperial Ephesus – and yet nobody else in their day and generation thought of doing anything of the kind. If they ever did, their grottoes are all gone, and I suppose we ought to wonder at the peculiar marvel of the preservation of these I speak of....It is an imposture – this grotto stuff – but it is one that all men ought to thank the Catholics for. Wherever they ferret out a lost locality made holy by some scriptural event, they straightway build a massive – almost imperishable – church there, and preserve the memory of that locality for the gratification of future generations.

*First Sight of Jerusalem*

At last, away in the middle of the day, ancient bits of wall and crumbling arches began to line the way – we toiled up one more hill, and every pilgrim and every sinner swung his hat on high! Jerusalem!

Perched on its eternal hills, white and domed and solid, massed together and hooped with high grey walls, the venerable city gleamed in the sun. So small! Why, it was no larger than an American village of 4,000 inhabitants, and no larger than an ordinary Syrian city of 30,000. Jerusalem numbers only 14,000 people.

We dismounted and looked, without speaking a dozen sentences, across the wide intervening valley for an hour or more; and noted those prominent features of the city that pictures make familiar to all men from their school-days till their death....

I record it here as a notable but not discreditable fact that not even our pilgrims wept. I think there was no individual in the party whose brain was not teeming with thoughts and images and memories evoked by the grand history of the venerable city that lay before us, but still among us all was no 'voice of them that wept'.

There was no call for tears. Tears would have been out of place. The thoughts Jerusalem suggest are full of poetry, sublimity and, more than all, dignity....

Just after noon, we entered these narrow, crooked streets by the ancient and famed Damascus Gate, and now for several hours I have been trying to comprehend that I am actually in the illustrious old city where Solomon dwelt, where Abraham held converse with the Deity, and where walls still stand that witnessed the spectacle of the Crucifixion.

A fast walker could go outside the walls of Jerusalem and walk entirely round the city in an hour. I do not know how else to make one understand how small it is. It is as knobby with countless little domes as a prison door with bolt-heads. Every house has from one to half a dozen of these white plastered domes of stone, broad and low, sitting in the centre of, or in a cluster upon, the flat roof. Wherefore, when one looks down from an eminence upon the compact mass of houses (so closely crowded together, in fact, that there is no appearance of streets at all, and so the city looks solid), he sees the knobbiest town in the world, except Constantinople. It looks as if it might be roofed, from centre to circumference, with inverted saucers. The monotony of the view is interrupted only by the great Mosque of Omar, the Tower of Hippicus, and one or two other buildings that rise into commanding prominence.

The houses are generally two storeys high, built strongly of masonry, whitewashed or plastered outside, and have a cage of wooden lattice-work projecting in front of every window. To reproduce a Jerusalem street, it would only be necessary to up-end a chicken-coop and hang it before each window in an alley of American houses.

The streets are roughly and badly paved with stone, and are tolerably crooked – enough so to make each street appear to close together constantly and come to an end about a hundred yards ahead of the pilgrim as long as he chooses to walk in it. Projecting from the top of the lower storey of many of the houses is a very narrow porch-roof or shed, without supports from below, and I have several times seen cats jump across the street from one shed to the other when they were out calling. The cats could have jumped double the distance without extraordinary exertion. I mention these things to give an idea of how narrow the streets are. Since a cat can jump across them without the least inconvenience, it is hardly necessary to state that such streets are too narrow for carriages. These vehicles cannot navigate the Holy City.

The population of Jerusalem is composed of Moslems, Jews, Greeks, Latins, Armenians,

*A typical Jerusalem street (photo by Frank Mason Good)*

Syrians, Copts, Abyssinians, Greek catholics and a handful of Protestants. One hundred of the latter sect are all that dwell now in this birthplace of Christianity. The nice shades of nationality comprised in the above list, and the languages spoken by them, are altogether too numerous to mention. It seems to me that all the races and colours and tongues of the earth must be represented among the 14,000 souls that dwell in Jerusalem. Rags, wretchedness, poverty and dirt, those signs and symbols that indicate the presence of Moslem rule more surely than the crescent-flag itself, abound. Lepers, cripples, the blind and the idiotic assail you on every hand, and they know but one word of but one language apparently – the eternal 'bakshish'. To see the numbers of maimed, malformed and diseased humanity that throng the Holy Places and obstruct the gates, one might suppose that the ancient days had come again, and that the angel of the Lord was expected to descend at any moment to stir the waters of Bethesda. Jerusalem is mournful and dreary and lifeless. I would not desire to live here.

## Swimming in the Dead Sea

Daylight came, soon after we got under way, and in the course of an hour or two we reached the Dead Sea. Nothing grows in the flat, burning desert around it but weeds and the Dead Sea apple the poets say is beautiful to the eye, but crumbles to ashes and dust when you break it. Such as we found were not handsome, but they were bitter to the taste. They yielded no dust. It was because they were not ripe, perhaps.

The desert and the barren hills gleam painfully in the sun around the Dead Sea, and there is no pleasant thing or living creature upon it or about its borders to cheer the eye. It is a scorching, arid, repulsive solitude. A silence broods over the scene that is depressing to the spirits. It makes one think of funerals and death.

The Dead Sea is small. Its waters are very clear, and it has a pebbly bottom, and is shallow for some distance out from the shores. It yields quantities of asphaltum; fragments of it lie all about its banks; this stuff gives the place something of an unpleasant smell.

All our reading has taught us to expect that the first plunge into the Dead Sea would be attained with distressing results – our bodies would feel as if they were suddenly pierced by millions of red-hot needles, the dreadful smarting would continue for hours; we might even look to be blistered from head to foot, and suffer miserably for many days. We were disappointed. Our eight sprang in at the same time that another party of pilgrims did, and nobody screamed once. None of them ever did complain of anything more than slight pricking sensation in places where their skin was abraded, and then only for a short time. My face smarted for a couple of hours, but it was partly because I got it badly sun-burned while I was bathing, and stayed in so long that it became plastered with salt.

No; the water did not blister us; it did not cover us with a slimy ooze, and confer upon us an atrocious fragrance; and I could not discover that we smelt really any worse than we have always smelt since we have been in Palestine. It was only a different kind of smell, but not conspicuous on that account....

It was a funny bath. We could not sink. One could stretch himself at full length on his back, with his arms on his breast, and all of his body above a line drawn from the corner of his jaw past the middle of his side, the middle of his leg and through his ankle-bone, would remain out of water. He could lift his head clear out, if he chose. No position can be retained for long; you lose your balance and whirl over, first on your back and then on your face, and so on. You can lie comfortably on your back, with your head out, and your legs in front from your knees down, by steadying yourself with your hands. You can sit with your knees drawn up to your chin and your arms clasped around them, but you are bound to turn over presently because you are top-heavy in that position. You can stand up straight in water that is over your head, and from the middle of your breast upward you will not be wet. But you cannot remain so. The water will soon float your feet to the surface....Some of us bathed for more than an hour and then came out coated with salt till we shone like icicles. We scrubbed it off with a coarse towel and rode off with a splendid brand-new smell, though it was one which was not any more disagreeable than those we have been for several weeks enjoying. It was the variegated villainy and novelty of it that charmed us. Salt crystals glitter in the sun about the shores of the lake. In places they coat the ground like a brilliant crust.

When I was a boy I somehow got the impression that the River Jordan was 4,000 miles long and thirty-five miles wide. It is only ninety miles long and so crooked that a man does not know which side of it he is on half the time. It is not any wider than Broadway in New York. There is the Sea of Galilee and this Dead Sea – neither of them twenty miles long or thirteen miles wide. And yet when I was in Sunday day-school I thought they were 60,000 miles in diameter....

### Final reflections

The commonest sagacity warns me that I ought to tell the customary pleasant lie and say I tore myself reluctantly away from every noted place in Palestine. Everybody tells that, but with as little ostentation as I may, I doubt the word of every he who tells it. I could take a dreadful oath that I have never heard any one of our forty pilgrims say anything of the sort, and they are as worthy and as sincerely devout as any that come here. They will say it when they get home fast enough, but why should they not? They do not wish to array themselves against all the Lamartines and Grimeses in the world. It does not stand to reason that men are reluctant to leave places where the very life is almost badgered out of them by importunate swarms of beggars and pedlars, who hang in the strings to one's sleeves and coat-tails, and shriek and shout in his ears, and horrify his vision with the ghastly sores and malformations they exhibit. One is *glad* to get away....No; it is the neat thing to say you were reluctant, and then append the profound thoughts that 'struggled for utterance' in your brain; but it is the true thing to say that you were not reluctant, and found it impossible to think at all – though in good sooth it is not respectable to say it, and not poetical either.

We do not think in the holy places; we think in bed, afterwards, when the glare, and the noise, and the confusion are gone, and in fancy we revisit alone the solemn monuments of the past, and summon the phantom pageants of an age that has passed away.

# COMTE DE VOLNEY

## 1757–1820

Comte de Volney

*Constantin François Chasseboeuf, Comte de Volney, was born at Craon, in Mayenne, and studied
medicine in Paris. Having been left a small inheritance in 1781, he determined to travel to Egypt
and Syria in order to report on the people and their customs. He set off at the end of 1782 and
spent the next three years abroad – living in Cairo for seven months, learning Arabic among the
Druses for eight months and travelling throughout Syria for a year. On his return to France, he
published a two-volume account of his journey,* Travels through Syria and Egypt, *in 1787. A
zealous reformer, Volney was elected to the Constituent Assembly in 1789, but was later thrown
into prison and not released until Robespierre's downfall. In 1791 he wrote his most famous work,*
Les Ruines, ou Méditations sur les révolutions des empires *(translated in 1795), inspired by the
ruins of Palmyra which became the occasion for reflection on the rise, progress and decline of ancient
civilizations and the prospect for modern ones. Professor of History at the short-lived Ecole
Normale, he spent the years 1795–8 in the United States collecting material for his* Tableau de
climat et du sol. *He was made a senator, a count and a commander of the Légion d'honneur by
Napoleon and a peer by Louis XVII.*

*Of the Manners and Characters of the Inhabitants of Syria*

Of all the subjects of observation any country affords, the moral character of its inhabitants is unquestionably the most important; but it must likewise be acknowledged, it is at the same time the most difficult: for it is not sufficient to make a barren enquiry into facts; the essential object is to investigate their various causes and relations; to discover the open or secret, the remote or immediate springs, which produce in men those habits of action we call manners, and the uniform disposition of mind we name character....

When an European arrives in Syria, or indeed in any part of the Eastern world, what appears most extraordinary to him, in the exterior of the inhabitants, is the almost total opposition of their manners to our own: it seems as if some premeditated design had determined to produce an infinity of the most striking contrasts between the people of Asia and those of Europe. We wear short and close dresses; theirs are long and ample. We suffer our hair to grow, and shave the beard; they let the beard grow, and shave the head. With us, to uncover the head is a mark of respect; with them, a naked head is a sign of folly. We salute in an inclined posture; they upright. We pass our lives erect; they are almost continually seated....To the bulk of travellers these contrasts only appear whimsical; but it may be interesting to enquire into the causes of so great a diversity of habits, in men who have the same wants, and in nations which appear to have one common origin.

Another distinguishing characteristic, no less remarkable, is that religious exterior observable in the countenances, conversation and gestures of the inhabitants of Turkey. In the streets, everyone appears with his string of beads. We hear nothing but emphatical exclamations of *Ya Allah!* O God! *Allah akbar!* God most great! *Allah taala!* God most high! Every instant the ear is struck with a profound sigh, or noisy eructation which follows the pronouncing of some one of the ninety-nine epithets of God; such as *Ya rani!* Source of riches! *Ya fobhan!* O most to be praised!...These men then are very devout, says the reader? Yes, but without being the better in consequence of this devotion, for I have already observed their zeal is no other than a spirit of jealousy, and contradiction arising from the diversity of religions; since in the Christian a profession of his faith is a bravado, an act of independence; and in the Mohammedan, an act of superiority and power. This devoutness, therefore, merely the offspring of pride and profound ignorance, is no better than a fanatic superstition, and the source of innumerable disorders.

There is still another characteristic in the exterior of the orientals, which attracts attention of an observer: I mean their grave and phlegmatic air in everything they do, or say. Instead of that open and cheerful countenance, which we either naturally possess or assume, their behaviour is serious, austere and melancholy; they rarely laugh, and the gaiety of the French appears to them a fit of delirium. When they speak it is without gestures and without passion; they listen without interrupting you; they are silent for whole days together, and by no means pique themselves on supporting conversation. If they walk; it is always leisurely, and on business; they have no idea of our troublesome activity, and our walks backwards and forwards for amusement. Continually seated, they pass whole days musing, with their legs crossed, their pipes in their mouths, and almost without changing their attitude. It should seem as if motion were a punishment to them, and that, like the Indians, they regard inaction as essential to happiness....

I have said that orientals, in general, have a grave and phlegmatic exterior .... Were the climate or the soil the radical cause of this, the effect would be the same in every individual. But that is not the case: under this general character, there are a thousand peculiar minute varieties in different classes and individuals, arising from their situation, relative to the influence of government, which differs in its effects on these classes....Thus we observe that the peasants subject to the Turks are more gloomy than those of the tributary countries; that the inhabitants of the country are less gay than those of the towns; and that those on the coast are more cheerful than such as dwell at a greater distance from it; that in the same town, the professors of the law are more serious than the military, and there again more so than the people. We may even remark that, in the great cities, the people have much of that dissipated and careless air they usually have with us; because there, as well as here, inured to suffering from habit, and devoid of reflection from ignorance, they enjoy a kind of security. Having nothing to lose, they are in no dread of being plundered. The merchant, on the contrary, lives in a state of perpetual alarm, under the double apprehension of acquiring no more, and losing what he possesses. He trembles lest he should attract the attention of rapacious authority, which he would consider an air of satisfaction as a proof of opulence, and the signal for extortion. The same dread prevails throughout the villages, where each peasant is afraid of exciting the envy of his equals, and the avarice of the aga and his soldiers. In such a country, where the subject is perpetually watched by a despoiling government, he must assume a serious countenance for the same reason that he wears ragged clothes, and makes a public parade of eating cheese and olives....

## Of the City of Jerusalem

Two days' journey to the south of Nablus, following the course of the mountains, which at every step become more barren and rocky, we arrive at a town, which, like many others already mentioned, presents a striking example of the vicissitude of human affairs: when we behold its walls levelled, its ditches filled up, and all its buildings embarrassed with ruins, we scarcely can believe we view that celebrated metropolis, which, formerly, withstood the efforts of the most powerful empires, and, for a time, resisted the arms of Rome herself; though, by a whimsical change of fortune, its ruins now receive her homage and reverence; in a word, we with difficulty recognize Jerusalem. Still more are we astonished at its ancient greatness, when we consider its situation, amid a rugged soil, destitute of water, and surrounded by dry channels of torrents and steep heights. Remote from every great road, it seems neither to have been calculated for a considerable mart of commerce, nor the centre of a great consumption. It overcame, however, every obstacle, and may be adduced as a proof of what popular opinions may effect in the hands of an able Legislature, or when favoured by happy circumstances. The same opinions still preserve to this city its feeble existence. The renown of its miracles perpetuated in the East, invites and retains a certain number of inhabitants within its walls. Mohammedans, Christians, Jews, without distinction of sects, all make it a point of honour to see, or to have seen, what they denominate the noble and holy city. To judge from the respect the inhabitants profess for the sacred places it contains, we should be ready to imagine there is not in the world a more devout people; but this has not prevented them from acquiring, and well deserving, the reputation of the vilest people in Syria, without excepting those even in Damascus. Their number is supposed to amount to 12,000 or 14,000.

Jerusalem has from time to time had governors of its own, with the title of Pashas; but it is in general, as at this day, a dependency of Damascus, from which it receives a Motfallam, or deputy governor. This Motfallam farms it and receives the revenues arising from the Miri, the customs, and especially from the follies of the Christian inhabitants. To conceive the nature of this last article, it must be understood, that the different communions of schismatic, and catholic Greeks; Armenians, Copts, Abyssinians and Franks, mutually

*The Greek Church of the Holy Sepulchre, by David Roberts – one of the Christian sects vying for possession of the Holy Places*

envying each other the possession of the holy places, are continually endeavouring to outbid one another in the price they offer for them to the Turkish governors. They are constantly aiming to obtain some privilege for themselves, or to take it from their rivals. And each sect is perpetually informing against the other for irregularities. Has a church been clandestinely repaired; or a procession extended beyond the usual limits; has a pilgrim entered by a different gate from that customary: all these are subjects of accusation to the government, which never fails to profit by them, by fines and extortions. Hence those hatreds, and that eternal jangling, which prevail between the different convents; and the adherents of each communion. The Turks, to whom every dispute produces money, are, as we may imagine, far from wishing to put an end to them. They all, in whatever station, derive some advantage from these quarrels: some sell their protection, others their interest. Hence a spirit of intrigue and cabal, which has diffused venality through every class; and hence perquisites for the Motfallam, which annually amount to upwards of 100,000 piastres. Every pilgrim pays him an entrance fee of ten piastres, and another for an escort for the journey to the Jordan, without reckoning the fines imposed in consequence of the imprudencies committed by these strangers during their stay. Each convent pays him so much for the privilege of processions, and so much for all repairs they undertake, besides presents on the accession of a new superior, or a new Motfallam; not to speak of private gratifications to obtain secret trifles they solicit; all which is carried to a great length among the Turks, who are as well versed in the art of squeezing money as the most able law practitioners in Europe. Besides all this, the Motfallam collects duties on the exportation of certain singular commodities from Jerusalem, I mean beads, relics, sanctuaries, crosses, passions, agnus deis, scapularies, etc., of which near 300 chests are sent off annually. The fabrication of these utensils of piety procures subsistence for the greatest part of the Christian and Mohammedan families of Jerusalem and its neighbourhood....To this the convents join another not less important article of traffic, the visits of the pilgrims. It is well known that at all times the devout curiosity of visiting the holy places has conducted Christians of every country to Jerusalem. There was even a time when the ministers of religion taught it was indispensably necessary to salvation, and this pious zeal pervading Europe gave rise to the Crusades. Since their unfortunate issue, the zeal of the Europeans cooling every day, the number of pilgrims has diminished; and is now reduced to a few Italian, Spanish and German monks, but the case is different with the orientals. Faithful to the spirit of past times, they continue to consider the journey to Jerusalem as a work of the greatest merit. They are even scandalized at the relaxation of the Franks in this respect and say they have all become heretics or infidels. Their priests and monks, who find their advantage in this fervor, do not cease to promote it....

We may suppose that so great a multitude, residing at Jerusalem for five or six months, must leave behind them considerable sums; and reckoning only 1,500 persons, at 100 pistoles each, we shall find they cannot expend less than a million and a half livres (£52,500). Part of this money is paid to the inhabitants and merchants for necessaries.... Another part goes to the governor and his subalterns, and the remainder is the profit of the convents. Great complaints are made of the improper use the schismatics make of this money, and their luxury is spoken of as a great scandal .... The Armenians and the Franks are much more modest; with the former, who are poor, it is a virtue of necessity; but with the latter, who are not so, it is prudence....

# CHARLES WARREN

## 1840–1927

*Charles Warren*

*Charles Warren was born in Bangor, Wales, in 1840. He joined the Royal Engineers in 1857 and in 1867 was appointed to head the Palestine Exploration Fund's team for its second season of surveying the Holy Land. He was given the task not only of surveying and making maps, but of establishing the location of disputed areas of biblical Jerusalem, especially the controversial position of the 'second wall' of Herod's time – that of the area forming the Temple Mount and the site of the Holy Sepulchre. Within a few months of excavating, Warren soon reconstructed the topography of much of the Temple Mount as it was in Herod's day. The results of his excavations were published in Underground Jerusalem (1876). He later wrote two further books on Jerusalem – Temple and Tomb (1880) and Jerusalem (1884, with Conder). From 1876 to 1877, he was employed in Griqualand West, commanded the Diamond Fields Horse in the Kaffir war of 1877–8, took part in the Egyptian campaign in 1882 and successfully commanded the Bechuanaland expedition of 1884–5. In later life he served as chief commissioner of the London Metropolitan Police and, after being promoted to lieutenant-general in 1897, he commanded the 5th division during the South African war from 1899 to 1900. He was awarded the KCMG in 1882 and appointed a general in 1904.*

*Early Excavations in Jerusalem*

My interview with Izzet Pasha over, I had lost no time in commencing work at the water passages, under the eastern of the two ancient gates of Herod's Temple, facing the midday sun. Fortune favoured our enterprise, and in a few hours an old parting wall in the rock-hewn aqueduct yielded to our efforts, and we found ourselves in the substructures of the Temple itself; among the piers supporting the vast vaults, called the Stables of Solomon; below where once stood the palace of that great king. Our progress through these passages had been rapid, but unhappily the hammer-blows, resounding through the hollow walls in so unwonted a manner, alarmed the modern representative of the High Priest. Infuriate with anger, the fine old sheikh would listen to no reasoning: but repairing to the south-east angle of the old Temple enclosure, mounted its battlements and summoned the Sheikh of Siloam to stand forth and answer for his misdeeds. With full turban and long flowing robes, edges tipped with fur, the old man stood, on the edge of the steep masonry, stamping his feet with rage and bellowing imprecations....

Subsequently, when I became on very excellent terms with the sheikh of the mosque, I asked him why he had behaved in such an outrageous manner ... injuring his own prospects as well as those of others. His reasons were many and various but they appeared principally to be, that the military pasha had previously sent for him and told him he should he deposed from his post if he gave us any assistance....

I went to see Izzet Pasha, but he was obdurate: saying I had no vizierial letter, and that the military pasha was very strict in his religious views; after considerable difficulty I arranged with him for the nonce to work at some distance from the Sanctuary.

I commenced work at one of the old gates of the first wall, near the English cemetery, and also along the third wall near the Damascus Gate: but it was evident that there was a desire to tire me out and make the excavation impossible; seeing this, I made a long list of places, and whenever we were stopped in one, we commenced work in another, until the pasha became quite exhausted in his objections, and then, having baffled him, I returned to the original places; this disagreeable kind of work continued for some weeks until I had got a firm footing in Jerusalem.

One of the chief fears of the military pasha was that I might suddenly appear under the leaves of his 'Palm Tree', and in order to secure it, all the time I was at Jerusalem an additional night guard was kept in the mosque itself, to prevent the 'Mole', as I was called, making his way in. Also an unaccountable rumour arose that I had arrived on a very sinister mission; that I was to place small packets of gunpowder around the sanctuary walls at a great depth, and then, when they had grown or developed during the course of years into barrels of gunpowder, I was again to come and fire them, in order to destroy the grand old walls. Whether this insane notion was promulgated by the military pasha, I cannot say, but its object evidently was to cause dislike among the people to our excavations.

Fortunately I commenced to open up a deep cleft in the rock near the Russian Buildings, to the north of the city, and this, together with our actually finding water under the great causeway, changed the opinions of the people, and many of the fanatics then allowed that we might be looking for water; but the pashas could never look with favour on the undertaking....

One of the early results of our excavations this October was the demonstration that Robinson's Arch never led across the central valley to the Upper City, and the discovery of the remains of the Xystus....

Our first shaft in the line of the Royal Cloister, instead of finding the remains of any bridge, exposed the walls of this Xystus, which appears to have consisted of a triple series of vaults, side by side, stretching north from a point opposite the south-west angle, as far as the great causeway on which the first wall was built across the valley; to the west of this was the stadium 600 feet in length in which the games were carried on, partially paved with white marble, and farther west were the seats of the spectators, ranged along the rising hill of the Upper City. This place of exercise differed from that more generally used in other cities, in that the stadium and Xystus were parallel one to the other: but this is to be accounted for by the nature of the ground, which would not admit of other arrangement....

Pursuing our mining operations across the valley to east, as we advanced within 100 feet of the Royal Cloisters, we came upon a tank, one wall of which was of very solid masonry, standing on the rock, part of which was scarped; this gave no clue at first, but afterwards, on comparing distances, this wall appeared to be the second pier of that grand bridge; farther on we mined our way, until, when at a distance of fifty-three feet from the Temple wall, we made the grand discovery, which was to throw all controversy on Jerusalem topography into a new groove, to upset many hitherto much cherished theories; it was no less than the pier of that great arch, the springing of which above ground Dr Robinson had first perceived to be anything more than a projecting stone in the face of the wall....This pier we found deep down in the accumulated earth, built on the rock, of magnificent stones, from sixty to eighty tons in weight, of which three courses still remain perfect: courses similar to those in the Temple wall and evidently of Herodian architecture.

Getting on to and over the remains of this pier, still mining through the crumbling earth, we examined its eastern side and discovered, lying pell mell, just as they fell on the old marble pavement (some forty feet below the present surface of the ground), the enormous voussoirs of the old arch, which once supported the magnificent ascent from the Xystus to the Royal Cloister; thrown down by Titus's engineers in their destruction of the city after its capture.

Now we have ascertained that this arch was not one of series, reaching across the valley to the Upper City, and so far Dr Robinson was mistaken; this arch supported the Propylaea leading from the valley into the Royal Cloister, a noble approach to this grand arcade.

But it was not merely this as an isolated fact which is so important, but the light it throws on the topography generally; for if this was not the bridge stretching across the valley, and it is not; where was that bridge? It could be no other than that at Wilson's Arch....

I have mentioned that the stones of this arch lay on the marble pavement; but this is not at the bottom of the valley: the pier is built upon a rocky cliff falling steeply to the east, so that the marble pavement is twenty-two feet above the rocky foundation of the Temple wall; the space between being filled with rubbish. All the wall above this pavement was once exposed to view, the stones are of great size, well cut and like those at the Wailing Place; but those below the pavement were never intended to be seen. They have well-cut marginal drafts and are beautifully jointed, but inside the draft all is rough; and this is the case, not only under the arch itself, but also round the corner to the south, for many feet to the east. Now the tale this tells is most emphatic. It informs us that this portion of the Temple wall was not built until the valley had begun to fill up with rubbish; until late in the days of Jerusalem, until the time of Herod.

...The conclusion is irresistible: the other portions were built first, they are the remains of the Temple and palace of the Kings of Judah; and this portion of Robinson's Arch was added by King Herod when he enlarged the Temple, and when the valley had commenced to fill up....

I now mention another point. We sunk a shaft below this pavement among the voussoirs, reached the bottom of the scarp, felt our way across to the foundations of the

*Illustration of Warren discovering the voussoir of the old arch which once supported the ascent from the Xystus to the Royal Cloister*

wall, and just before reaching it found a rock aqueduct of very ancient construction, running north and south – the brook that flowed through the midst of the land. The aqueduct is actually cut in two by the Temple wall, the addition of Herod, showing how comparatively recent must be this wall. Add to this, let me observe, that this aqueduct is by no means placed at the bottom of the valley; for this valley still slopes down to the east under the Temple wall for eight feet. What strong evidence this is against Mr Fergusson's theory: the Temple was built on a hill, but this wall stretches over the very bottom of the valley. Can anyone conceive that the lowest part of a valley could have been selected for the site of the Temple? We have record that it was not, but was on a hill: this cannot then be the old Temple wall; it can be no other than the addition by Herod....

*Excavating inside the Temple Area*

It will perhaps be recollected, it was once thought probable that there was a succession of vaults on the south-west side of the Temple area similar to those on the south-east, and that the double tunnel, leading from the Double Gate, was one of them. There seems, however, now no likelihood of this; indeed, if there were such vaults, why should not there also be openings from them as there are on the other side? I persuaded those most interested to let me excavate in this Double Passage, which is one of the most sacred of the Moslem praying places; being the presumed site of Solomon's Palace....

While Sergeant Birtles and I cut our way through the strong walls of this double passage, our faithful Moslem friends kept guard inside and outside and diverted the attention of those who wanted to come there to pray. In the sanctuary live, for the protection of the place, certain Africans or Nubian men, of the most bigoted nature, who think nothing of life or the loss of it; to these the good keeping of the sanctuary is left; and their fanaticism knows no bounds; but I found means to be friendly with these people.

They once ate a very large pet lizard of mine which I wanted to send home to the Zoological Gardens in London, and I took advantage of the occurrence to make friends with them, so that instead of coming and throwing stones at me when I entered the Temple area by myself, they would stand up and deferentially salaam. However, I never attempted to test their good feeling too far, and on this occasion they were given a hint that they might obtain a smell of grilled lizard if they went in a certain direction. This was enough for them; they are greedily fond of the large lizard, which happens to be my namesake, Warren, and were thus out of our way.

The blows of our hammers resounded in the vaults, and soon our Moslem friends got into the greatest fright lest all would be discovered: however, we were in for it; if we were to be set upon and eaten up instead of the lizard, we might as well complete our work first. Accordingly, whenever we were implored to stop, we made the more noise until our friends lay in a corner tearing their beards and plucking at their garments in the greatest state of agonized terror. It was very exciting; we had visions of wonderful vaults beyond us with sculptures and what not; but, when we had got through the wall, we only found earth against it with rough face, or rather no face. There are certainly no vaults to the east of the Standing Place of Elias....

We now changed over to the west side of the double tunnel.... This time we thought we must get hold of some new fact, and so we did, but only a negative one; namely, that the vaults do not extend further to the west – and so we had put our lives in the greatest peril for these negative results.... As soon as we had done the work, we got our tools out of the passage in the same secret manner we had brought them in, and appeared under the clear winter sky – two very grubby-looking mortals, for we had been groping head foremost in the earth. We could not go outside in such a state, and measures were taken to clean us up a little. It was very exciting, for by this time our Nubian friends had found that in the hunt after the lizard they were on a false scent, and that the lizard (Warren) they should have been after was in the double tunnel, and came back to find out what was going on; but we had completed our work and were not to be torn in pieces on this occasion.

# WILLIAM WILDE

## 1815–76

*William Wilde, 1847 (engraving by T.H. Maguire)*

*William Robert Wilde was born in the small town of Castlerea, Co. Roscommon, in Ireland. He began his surgical studies in Dublin in 1832 and obtained his diploma as a surgeon in 1837. He then spent nine months in charge of an invalid patient on board a yacht, which sailed through the Mediterranean. It was during this journey that Wilde also visited Egypt and Palestine. His first book, the account of these travels –* Narrative of Journey to Madeira, Teneriffe and along the Shores of the Mediterranean *– was published in 1840. He subsequently returned to his studies, specializing in aural and opthalmic medicine, and in 1844 he founded a hospital in Dublin, St Marks, which was the first to treat the afflictions of these organs in Ireland. His reputation soon grew, and he founded and edited the* Dublin Quarterly Journal of Medical Science, *and wrote the earliest textbooks in his field,* Epidemic Opthalmia *(1851) and* Aural Surgery *(1853). When a census was undertaken in Ireland in 1851, Wilde was appointed the census commissioner to organize the collection of medical information. His statistics on the incidence of deafness, blindness and diseases of the ears and eyes were the first ever to be completed in Ireland. As a result of this work he was appointed Surgeon Occulist to the Queen in Ireland in 1863 and, a year later, was knighted. His interests were wide-ranging and, amongst others, he wrote a short book on Swift, a book on Irish superstitions and a catalogue of the antiquities in the collection of the National Museum of Ireland. The father of Oscar Wilde, Sir William died in Dublin in 1876.*

*Bethlehem*

On the bright sunny morning of the 23rd we procured horses, and leaving the city by the Bethlehem or Sion Gate, set forward to visit the place of our Lord's nativity. We crossed over the valley of Gihon, above the large cistern or enclosure in this ravine called the lower pool of Gihon, and proceeded along the verge of the long irregular hill from which the valley derives its name.... The distance from Jerusalem to Bethlehem is about six miles, or not two hours' ride, and Father Benjamin kindly furnished us with a letter of introduction to a brother friar of the convent there. For the first mile and a half the road passed over tolerably level plain, with some vegetation and several cultivated patches.

Shortly after leaving the city we met several flocks of sheep, preceded by their shepherds walking slowly towards Jerusalem, and at once the full force of all the beautiful imagery, and the many touching similes derived from such scenes and associations, and so often alluded to in Scripture, came vividly before me. These Arab shepherds, clad in the turbans and simple abbas worn by their class, and carrying a wooden crook in their hands, walked in front.... After the sheep came some young goats and lambs, and the whole procession closed with about two dozen of old, patriarchal looking goats who brought up the rear.... These shepherds are often to be seen about sunset slowly approaching the city from all sides, to seek shelter for their flocks, during the night, in some of the deep valleys by which it is surrounded, carrying the lambs in their bosoms....

It is probably to such shepherds as these that the angel announced the glad tidings of the Saviour's birth....

As we approached the village, the scenery improved; the path winds through olive yards and corn fields, such as, in all probability, the Saviour often traversed. Bethlehem is beautifully situated and does not require even the hallowed scenes, and the associations connected with its history – though they certainly heighten its effect and give it an additional interest – to arrest the attention of the traveller and bid him gaze upon the picturesque hill that rises in parterres of vineyards, almond groves and fig plantations, watered by gentle rivulets that murmur through those terraces; and diversified by the tower and the wine-press.

On entering the town, we met a band of young girls going out to the neighbouring well, with their waterpots on their heads; and these, as well as the other females that we saw in Bethlehem, were some of the most beautiful of their sex that we met in the East....

Bethlehem is a straggling village with one broad and principal street; the houses have not domed roofs like those of Jerusalem and Ramlah, but are built, for the most part of clay and bricks, and every house is provided with an apiary, the beehives of which are constructed of a series of earthen pots, ranged on the house tops in the same manner as the wooden ones on the coast of Asia Minor. There are said to be about 3,000 inhabitants in this place, the greater part of whom are Arab Christians; for Ibrahim Pasha, finding that the Moslems were continually at war, had lately expelled the former, leaving the latter in peaceable possession of the village.

The inhabitants are nearly all engaged in the manufacture of those articles of sacred merchandise that supply the bazaars and warehouses in the Holy City; and no sooner was our party espied than we were beset by a multitude of bead hawkers and relic sellers, shouting aloud the respective holy powers and miraculous virtues of their different wares. Some of the articles wrought in mother-of-pearl are carved with considerable skill; more than we could expect to find in that distant land, and the workmanship of some would not disgrace the artists of our own country. One of these manufacturers, whose workshop I visited, informed me, that when a boy he had been sent by his parents to Spain, to be instructed in the trade.

In the street several Bedouin blacksmiths were at work. The rude and simple character of their temporary forges attracted our attention. The bellows which they employed was a most primitive instrument of its kind, being nothing more than an inflated goatskin bag, such as we read of being used by the early Greeks; and which in this instance was blown by the smith's wife pressing its sides together and then drawing them asunder to admit the air.

At the farthest extremity of the town is the Frank convent, at whose low massive door we alighted and were well received by the fraternity. We were first conducted into the cathedral of St Helena, a handsome, spacious hall, consisting of a central nave and aisles, separated from each other by rows of tall Corinthian pillars of grey marble, but much defaced by dirt and the remains of gaudy paintings. As there is no ceiling, the lofty roof is exposed to view; and although composed of the last of the cedars of Lebanon, it is still in a state of good preservation and affords a fine specimen of architecture of its day. The chapel at the upper end of the hall is now separated from it by a wall, as it was considered too expensive to keep up the whole; and the centre has a most cold, lonely and desolate appearance....The chapel belonging to this part of the building scarcely deserves our notice; but, the attendant monk placing in the right hand of each of us a large lighted taper, led us to the subterranean grotto, called the Chapel of the Nativity.

A flight of steps conducted us into an oblong apartment, on one side of which a small low crypt, said to be hewn out of the solid rock, was exhibited to us as the actual place of the Nativity. On one side of it is an altar with a silver plate, like to that at Calvary, and said to cover the spot on which the birth of the Saviour took place. Opposite to this, a niche in the wall contains a very handsome, polished white marble trough, like a sarcophagus, which is shown as the very manger in which the infant Jesus was laid!! This trough is on a level with the floor of the apartment, which is somewhat lower than that of the outer chamber. The niche in which it is placed contains a very good painting in the style of the Spanish school, representing the event. Another place in this little vault is shown as that in which the Magi presented their gifts and is also ornamented by a good painting. A number of silver lamps, suspended from the roof, are kept continually burning; the walls are ornamented with blue satin and brocade, which are now in rather a faded and torn condition, but patched with tawdry furniture calico. Can this be, in reality, the stable in which the infant Jesus was brought forth – and this the manger in which he was laid? I am constrained to say that I do not think they are: for the places shown as such are neither in accordance with the simple narrative of Scripture, nor at all analogous with the appearance that inns, or public caravansaries at present exhibit throughout the East; and it must be remembered that, in the never-changing manners and customs of this country, we have to this very day the same usages and habits that existed from the very earliest period that history records....

It is stated by the monks and all previous travellers have given insertion to the legend that the whole of this grotto is hewn out of the solid rock. This, from actual inspection, I can positively deny, for part of the tapestry having fallen from the roof I was enabled, much to the annoyance of the attendant friar, to examine it and found it arched with masonry. The chief objection to this place is its total dissimilarity to all other inns or resting places. The answer to this objection that 'it is by no means uncommon in these countries to use souterrains as habitations for both man and beast', cannot have any weight, or be taken as proof for the identity of the manger of Bethlehem; for the places that are thus alluded to were never formed for inns, but were originally tombs, which, having been rifled of their contents, became in turn resting places for occasional travellers, and their sarcophagi or stone troughs were converted into mangers ... and no other traveller has yet recorded a

*The Grotto of the Nativity, Bethlehem (aquatint published by Robert Bowyer, 1812)*

single instance in any country of a stable having been formed by excavating the rock beneath the surface; this, in particular, is so small that it could barely have held a donkey, which, in order to reach it, must have been led down a steep descent under ground. In order to determine this point I paid particular attention to the caravansaries of the different Eastern towns we visited. These places usually consist of a large square enclosure, surrounded by a range of buildings, the upper storeys of which are appropriated by the accommodation of travellers, and the lower and the courtyards itself for their beasts. It was in the latter of these in all probability the holy family had to take up their abode, the former being already so completely occupied as to afford them no room. To suppose that the place called the grotto of the nativity bears any similitude to the stable of an Eastern khan ... is truly preposterous....

## Mourning over the Stones of Jerusalem

One day during my stay, the whole [Jewish] congregation met upon the anniversary of the great earthquake of Safed, where so many of their brethren were destroyed. It was a touching sight, and one that years will not efface, to witness this mourning group and hear them singing the songs of David, in the full expressive language in which they were written,

*Jews praying at the Western Wall*

beneath Mount Zion, on which they were composed – and beneath those very walls that in other times rang with the same swelling chorus. But not now are heard the joyous tones of old; for here every note was swollen with a sigh, or broken with a song – the sighs of Judah's mourning maidens, the sobs and smothered groans of the patriarchs of Israel. And that heart must indeed be sadly out of tune, whose chords would not vibrate to the thrilling strains of Hebrew song, when chanted by the sons and daughters of Abraham, in their native city. Much as they venerate the very stones that now form the walls of this enclosure, they dare not set foot within its precincts; for the crescent of the Moslem is glittering from the minaret, and the blood-red banner of Mohammed is waving over their heads.

Were I asked what was the object of the greatest interest that I had seen, and the scene that made the deepest impression upon me, during my sojourn in other lands, I would say that it was a Jew mourning over the stones of Jerusalem. And what principle, what feeling is it, it may be asked, that can thus keep the Hebrew, through so many centuries, still yearning towards his native city – still looking forward to his restoration and the coming of the Messiah? Hope. Hope is the principle that supports the Israelite through all his sufferings – with oppression for his inheritance, sorrow and sadness for his certain lot; the constant fear of trials, bodily pain and mental anguish; without a country and without a home ... the power of man and even death itself cannot obliterate that feeling. It is hope that binds the laurel on the warrior's brow; that leads the soldier on to conquest, and bids him face the battle's dread array; that, pointing to the enjoyment of earthly honour and greatness in time, cheers man amidst every discouragement he may have to encounter and leads him to overcome every difficulty and obstacle for their attainment....It is the very life-boat of our existence – the oil that calms that sea of trouble, on which man launches at his birth....

# BIBLIOGRAPHY

The books listed below are those from which the extracts included in this book are taken. For other books on the Holy Land by the authors selected here, please see their biographical notes. An excellent general book for those who wish to read further is *The Zealous Intruders: The Western Rediscovery of Palestine* by Naomi Shepherd (London 1987).

Barclay, James Turner, *The City of the Great King* (Philadelphia 1858)

Bell, Lady (ed.), *The Letters of Gertrude Bell*, 2 vols (London 1927)

Buckingham, James Silk, *Travels in Palestine through the Countries of Bashan and Gilead* (London 1821)

Caroline of Brunswick, *Voyages and Travels of Her Majesty, Caroline Queen of Great Britain…by one of Her Majesty's Suite* (London 1821)

Chateaubriand, François René de, *Travels to Jerusalem*, 2 vols (London 1835)

Curzon, Robert, *Visits to Monasteries in the Levant* (London 1849)

Finn, James, *Stirring Times*, 2 vols (London 1878)

Hunt, William Holman, *Pre-Raphaelitism and the Pre-Raphaelite Brotherhood* 2 vols (London 1905)

Irby, Charles Leonard, and Mangles, James, *Travels in Egypt and Nubia, Syria and the Holy Land* (London 1844)

Kinglake, Alexander, *Eothen* (London 1846)

Kitchener, Horatio Herbert, reports to the *Palestine Exploration Fund's Quarterly Statement* (London 1875–7)

Lamartine, Alphonse de, *A Pilgrimage to the Holy Land*, 3 vols (London 1837)

Lawrence, T. E., and Woolley, C. Leonard, *The Wilderness of Zin* (London 1915)

Lear, Edward, 'A Leaf from the Journals of a Landscape Painter', *Macmillan's Magazine* (April 1897)

Loewe, Louis (ed.), *Diaries of Sir Moses and Lady Montefiore* (London 1890)

Macgregor, John, *The Rob Roy on the Jordan* (London 1870)

Meryon, Charles Lewis, *Travels of Lady Hester Stanhope … Narrated by her Physician*, 3 vols (London 1846)

Montefiore, Judith, *Notes from a Private Journal of a Visit to Egypt and Palestine…* (privately printed 1844)

Oliphant, Laurence, *Haifa, or Life in Modern Palestine* (London 1887)

Robinson, Edward, *Biblical Researches in Palestine, Mount Sinai and Arabia Petraea*, 3 vols (London 1842)

Rudolph, Crown Prince, *Travels in the East* (London 1884)

Stanley, Arthur Penrhyn, *Sermons Preached before His Royal Highness The Prince of Wales during his Tour in the East* (London 1863)

Stephens, John Lloyd, *Incidents of Travel in Egypt, Arabia Petraea and the Holy Land* (London 1856)

Thackeray, William Makepeace, *Notes on a Journey from Cornhill to Grand Cairo* (London 1846)

Tristram, Henry Baker, *The Land of Israel: A Journal of Travels in Palestine* (London 1865)

Twain, Mark, *The Innocents Abroad and the New Pilgrim's Progress* (Connecticut 1869)

Volney, F. C. Comte de, *Travels through Syria and Egypt, 1783–5*, 2 vols (London 1787)

Warren, Charles, *Underground Jerusalem* (London 1875)

Wilde, William, *Narrative of a Voyage…*, 2 vols (Dublin 1840)

# ACKNOWLEDGEMENTS

The editor and publisher would like to thank the following for their kind permission to use the photographs reproduced in the text: Mansell Collection, p.31; Mary Evans Picture Library, pp.67, 93, 109, 129, 134, 140; Multimedia Archives, pp.51, 61, 71, 75, 91, 107, 132; National Library of Ireland, p.150; National Portrait Gallery, pp.16, 21, 36, 48, 57, 62, 73, 78, 88, 114, 124; Palestine Exploration Fund, pp.14, 19, 24, 29, 34, 39, 42, 65, 81, 87, 96, 101, 103, 111, 117, 137, 143, 148, 154; The Print Room, pp.45, 53, 121, 127, 153; Royal Geographical Society, back cover and pp.11, 26, 83, 98, 145; Sotheby's, front cover; Weidenfeld Archives, p.104.